D0571713

The

GIFT

of

TIME

ALSO BY JORGE RAMOS

Dying to Cross

The Latino Wave

The Other Face of America

No Borders

The

GIFT

of

TIME

Letters *from a*
Father

⌇

Jorge Ramos

TRANSLATED FROM SPANISH
BY EZRA FITZ

wm

WILLIAM MORROW
An Imprint of HarperCollins*Publishers*

Writing letters . . . means showing your true self.

—FRANZ KAFKA

CONTENTS

CONTENTS

A CLARIFICATION
FOR THE READER

I wrote these letters for my kids. You'll be wondering, then, why did I decide to publish them; why didn't I keep them between my two children and me. To be honest, I may not have a completely appropriate reason. I'm crazy about my kids, and it makes me happy to share it.

Plus, if you take a peek at our little world, perhaps you'll see that our dilemmas and problems are not unlike your own. You'll encounter things that—by their very nature—are supremely personal. Nevertheless, I'm sure that you won't find them completely unfamiliar. Ultimately, I'm publishing these letters because I think that you and I have a lot in common.

So perhaps these letters are for you, after all.

The
GIFT
of
TIME

WHY I'M WRITING

Time is the longest distance between two places.

—TENNESSEE WILLIAMS

My Dearest Paola and Nicolás:

Life is so unbelievably short. Time together is a gift whose value we cannot discount.

I'm writing these letters to you before it's too late. No, don't worry; this isn't a good-bye. Actually, it's the opposite. These letters are an embrace. I'm writing to tell you things I've never told you before, or at least things that I haven't told you in their entirety. (It's not that I've been keeping secrets.)

These pages aren't going to be filled with advice, or at least I'm going to try and keep it on the light side—I know there can be little more irritating or aggravating than unsolicited opinions. Rather, I just want to recount some of the more important things I've learned in this half-century-long adventure—as a father, as a son and brother, as a journalist, as a foreigner, as a traveler— and to share them with you.

You might also be thinking that you've heard this all before, or that we could have discussed this ourselves over dinner some night. It's never a bad time to talk, and you two hang on my every word, right? But just in case your eager young minds don't always absorb every sage word uttered by your dear old dad, here is a backup.

⌇ **But just in case your eager young minds don't always absorb every sage word uttered by your dear old dad, here is a backup.**

Someday, I hope, you'll pick up these pages in search of the answer to some question: one of those unspoken gaps that always exist between fathers and children. I found myself left with many unanswered questions about my own father, and I don't want this to happen to you. My greatest fear isn't of dying—it's of dying before I've told you everything. I want you to know the special way in which you two have enriched my existence. Simply put, I want you to truly know how much I love you. I've accepted that it is possible this may come off a bit sappy. But it's inevitable that, from time to time, I'll stumble through the weeds of sentimentality in order to explain just how I feel. *Lo siento.*

I've heard fathers complain about how their lives were complicated by the birth of their children. For me, it was just the opposite. After each of you was born, my life became more simplified: I knew, during those moments, that nothing and no one was more important to me. And I've felt that way ever since. The rest is simply that: the rest. You do the choosing for me. I have inner peace knowing that the two of you come before anything else.

⌒ **After each of you was born, my life became more simplified: I knew, during those moments, that nothing and no
one was more important to me.**

Nicolás, as I'm sure you're tired of hearing by now, nothing
is more important to me than you and Paola. From time to time,
I'll smile at the look on your little face (your eyes looking up at
me as if I were crazy) when I repeat for the umpteenth time that
question-mantra that's so essential to me: "You know you're the
most important thing in my life, right?"

"You already said that, Dad," you tell me. And though hearing
that response calms me, a few days later, I'll find myself needing
to ask you yet again.

With you, Paola, I don't say that as much. Maybe it's because
you're older. There is no manual on how to be a parent, how often to say these things—and we've each had our hits and misses
during this chancy and beautiful adventure between first-time
fathers and their daughters.

Firstborn children, and I also speak as a firstborn, have the
honor of being the guinea pigs. We are test cases, experimental
subjects. This is not born of sometimes, it's because we're fum-
bling through the darkness. We don't know whether we're doing
a good job or not. So we stumble on through, though questions
abound. For example, you might ask me why I've chosen to publish this book, something so private? The three of us, I know, are
a shy group. Airing our own private laundry isn't for us.

Well, after twenty-five years of living externally, pursuing
the news, I've decided to give myself permission to pause for a
moment and take a look inside. And I've found myself to be a
very incomplete being. For years now, I've blocked or avoided

so many things that—at times—I don't even recognize myself. The letters that you're about to read have helped me to reconnect with my emotions and—someday—with you and with the people who surround and care about me. It's very affecting, almost a surprise, when you rediscover that spark buried deep within you. And now that I've found it, I'm not about to let it burn out again.

These letters contain everything that I've always wanted to say to you, everything I want you to remember. These letters are the result of the time that we've spent together. Unrepeatable time. And, above all, these letters are the clearest proof of the fact that my life is much, much grander thanks to you both.

Mountains of love,
Papá

Letter 2

ALMOST

⌒

Any life is made up of a single moment,
the moment in which a man finds out,
once and for all, who he is.

—JORGE LUIS BORGES

To my children, for every day that I spend with you:

On Wednesday, December 8, 2004, at 11:29 in the morning, I almost died. Almost. And in that one moment, I realized that I had arranged everything—a will and testament, bank accounts, insurance, precise instructions on whom to contact if I went missing—save for the most important thing of all: a testimony of how your lives have affected me.

I woke up that morning just like any other, took you to school, Nico, had breakfast (cereal, like always), read the paper, checked my e-mail, made a couple of phone calls, and got ready to go to the dentist. My colleagues at the office already knew I would be arriving a bit late.

Everything was normal. There was no breaking news that would require me to be at the TV station on time. When a story breaks, I have to cancel appointments, reschedule commitments, gather my passport, pack a suitcase, and rush to the office. There's no way to know what direction your life is about to take, whether for hours or weeks. Sometimes, there are news stories that change your life forever.

But that wasn't the case on this particular December morning. My dentist's Fort Lauderdale office was about a forty-minute drive from our old house in Coral Gables, and that morning I was running a little behind schedule. Not much—only five or ten minutes—but I hate being late. I don't like wasting other people's time, just as I don't like it when they waste mine.

I remember it perfectly. I got on the highway, heading north at around seventy miles per hour, pressing down a little more on the accelerator when there were no highway patrol cars in sight. I was hoping to make up those few extra minutes.

Despite having lived in the United States for over twenty years, these enormous three-, four-, and even five-lane highways never cease to amaze me as they merge and divide with one another via giant, multilevel bridges, forming perfect, unending bands across the landscape like marvelous concrete strings of spaghetti. When traffic is minimal, the speed limits seem to become arbitrary, enticing one to drive even faster, especially compared with the pothole-ridden streets in the town where I grew up.

These highway observations were what I was thinking about while on my way to my semiannual checkup, where I would have my teeth cleaned and be reprimanded for not flossing often enough. Even though there's nothing pleasant about opening your mouth for half an hour or so for the hygienist, it was far from unbearable. I was driving without concern.

It was a marvelous morning. The sun was shining with typical Floridian warmth. The windows were up. Even though I hate air conditioning, it is the only way to drive if you want to hear the radio. That's one of the things that I never liked about that old gray car: You couldn't open the windows without feeling like a hurricane was battering the back of your head, accompanied by an uncomfortable sound—like a plop—caused by the pressure changing in my left inner ear. *Plop.*

As usual, I was listening to one of Diane Rehm's wonderful interviews on NPR, but during one of her brief station breaks I looked down to search for a music station. I'd heard enough of that morning's guest and, besides, I wouldn't be able to finish the program anyway, as I was nearing my destination.

Soon, before I was able to find a song that I liked, I heard a loud noise approaching me. It was continuous and increasing quickly in volume. For a moment, I thought it was radio interference, and I changed from one station to another.

shshshSHSHSH!

It sounded as if someone were trying to hush me. I must have looked away from the road for a second, or maybe two. But when I looked back up at the road, at that very instant, I knew that I was going to die.

It sounded as if someone were trying to hush me. I must have looked away from the road for a second, or maybe two. But when I looked back up at the road, at that very instant, I knew that I was going to die.

An old, dark red van had lost control in an opposing lane of traffic and was hurtling directly toward me. It had already crossed the thirty-foot-wide grass median and was now heading the wrong way in my lane at breakneck speed. The collision would obviously be brutal—both our vehicles were traveling at highway speed—and I estimated that neither of us would have any chance at all of avoiding it.

I could see that the van's front left tire had blown out, which is probably why the driver had lost control. It was close enough now that I could read the license plate. It seemed like a tremendously stupid thing to be thinking about during my last seconds of life, but I couldn't help it. My mind was acting on its own. It had completely left me.

The approaching van was so incredibly surprising that I didn't even have a chance to slam on the brakes or swerve out of the way. "It's useless," I instinctively said to myself, resigned.

shshshSHSHSH!

The sound, like a runaway train, overwhelmed everything. I couldn't hear the music on the radio. Nevertheless, internally I felt a sense of steadfast calmness. I suppose that, given the situation, I should have thrown open my mouth and twisted my face into a mask of horror, but my muscles simply didn't react in that way. I'm sure that, at that moment, if I were to have looked into the mirror, I would have seen my face as completely expressionless.

The noise was louder now, like the impending attack of a monstrous bee.

Noise all around, and silence within.

Complete silence.

I thought for a moment that perhaps, with luck, the van would swerve and just miss me. But no. It was on a direct collision course!

All of this happened in a fraction of a second, but I felt like I was living it in slow motion. In moments like that, you can have thoughts running through your mind that would ordinarily take ten or twenty or however many times as long to process. I felt my heart beat twice. I don't know why, but that was it: exactly two heartbeats pounding beneath my sternum like waves breaking over rocks.

〜 **I felt my heart beat twice. I don't know why, but that was it: exactly two heartbeats pounding beneath my sternum like waves breaking over rocks.**

What's more, my sense of sight seemed suddenly heightened. I could see everything. Far better than with the glasses I wear for my incipient myopia. But it was no longer me who was watching the image of the oncoming van growing ever larger in my eyes. It was as if I had left my own body. I saw everything down to the last detail, through two black tunnels. My eyes had become telescopes. Nothing escaped them.

I saw that it was an old, rusted-out van, and it gave me some semblance of anger that I was about to be killed by an old bucket of bolts. I swear, that's what I was thinking about. The van's color had faded, it was filled with dents, and the front bumper was set at a very skewed angle. It looked a lot like the one owned by the painter who had worked with me through several house-to-house moves.

I hated that ruddy color, somewhere between purple and violet. The color of congealed blood.

We were just a few meters away now. The driver hadn't seen me, but I could see him. He was older than me, with gray hair and loose, wrinkled skin beneath his jaw. The dirty, white collar of his undershirt was folded over the neck of his sweater. I watched him trying hopelessly to gain control of his vehicle, but his wild jerking of the steering wheel didn't have the least effect on the car's direction on the road. It was almost comical. Desperately frustrated, he would throw the wheel in one direction only to have the van swerve the opposite way. I saw it all as if in super-slow motion.

The van was bearing down upon me. It was now a matter of moments.

I waited for the collision without even bracing myself. Why would I? I was going to die no matter what I did. Maybe, if I relaxed my body, I could somehow absorb some of the impact. I felt the seat belt across my chest. "It won't help a bit," I figured.

The van was coming at my left side—the driver's side—as if the driver had been aiming there all along . . . and was about to hit the bull's-eye.

shshshSHSHSH!

I took in half a breath, unhurried, blinked once, and still time seemed to draw out. I was about to leave this world without saying good-bye to my children. "How will they find out that I died? Who's going to tell them? What will they have for dinner tonight? What will Christmas be like?" I thought.

~ I took in half a breath, unhurried, blinked once, and still time seemed to draw out. I was about to leave this world without saying good-bye to my children. "How will they find out that I died? Who's going to tell them? What will they have for dinner tonight? What will Christmas be like?" I thought.

I also thought about work, though it pained me to do so. "They're expecting me at the office, and I'm not going to be there. They're going to be calling my cell phone, but I won't be picking up. Or would it even be working after the crash?" I just couldn't help but think about such trivial things. I was confounding the important—my children, my family—with absurd and unnecessary questions about my phone and the office. My mind was like a movie screen, and I had no control over what film was playing.

Without intending to, I started to think back to my earliest memories. "So this is what happens when you're about to die," I thought. But the video of my life seemed to be stuck on one particular point during my childhood where I was playing soccer in the yard.

It was all very strange: I could clearly see the van about to crash into me, but at the same time a series of images were flashing involuntarily through my mind with absolute clarity.

I cursed that morning's coincidences: "If I had spent just a little more (or less) time in the bathroom, this wouldn't be happening," I thought. Or one more spoonful of cereal for breakfast, one extra moment choosing what to wear, one more time rereading a headline in the morning paper . . . any little thing like that would have put me in a very different place than I was at that precise moment.

But I couldn't change a thing.

I imagined the mangled vehicle—as if it were one of those crude stories on a local news channel—and two paramedics lifting a body draped in a yellow blanket from it, carrying it with no real sense of urgency to a waiting ambulance.

That was me.

SHSHSHSHSHSH!

Inexplicably, the van shot past my driver's side window without touching me.

I heard that brutal droning sound, but it never quite made contact.

I felt my hair blown back as the van swept past me. I know, that was impossible since I had rolled up the windows, but there was an unmistakable breath of cold air that slapped me on my left cheek.

Death had passed by my side.

The trance had ended. The slow-motion camera returned to full speed.

In a flash, I was back in real time, and I stepped on the gas, leaving the out-of-control van behind me, and I became aware of the song on the radio. The images in my mind abruptly vanished.

I looked in my rearview mirror at the van, a Ford Econoline 150, my morbid curiosity waiting for the inevitable crash with another vehicle. Someone else instead of me was going to die. But the red spot that was the van continued to shrink into the distance until it was out of sight.

"Ahhhhhhh!" I shouted, alone there inside my car, feeling as if I were about to burst into tears as I pressed both of my hands to my face. I felt my skin: pallid, cold, lifeless, like cardboard. I thought for a moment about pulling over to the side of the road. I looked at my watch: 11:29 a.m. I didn't stop. I continued driving, though very slowly. My arms and legs were starting to tremble. I watched the overhanging signs for my doctor's exit number.

"I was saved," I thought.

But that wasn't it.

I wasn't saved.

From that moment on, nothing would be the same; something broke inside of me that day.

That wasn't the first time when I felt like my life was in danger. But for some reason, it was the most distinctive. And much more intense.

When I got out of the car, outside my dentist's office, I checked to see if there actually had been any contact between the two cars. But I was astounded again to find not so much as a scratch. Before I could sit down in the chair to have my teeth cleaned, I had to tell this to someone. I was already late, but I didn't care. So I called my friend and colleague Patsy Loris, whom you both know very well, and said, simply, "I almost died."

I entered the office and surrendered—willingly—to the hygienist. The scraping of my teeth and the bleeding of my gums were indisputable proof that I was alive. Alive. After all, pain is an affirmation of life. After the cleaning was over, I passed my tongue over my newly shining teeth and tried to return to my normal daily life. I got back in my car, checked to see if I had any messages on my cell phone, and turned the radio back on.

During the next few days, almost by accident, I began to feel overwhelmed, confused, and anxious. I couldn't stop thinking about the near-hit. Something was constricting my chest, all the way up to my throat. It was a rock that wouldn't let me breathe. I tried, as I had in the past, to downplay the incident. "I've been through worse experiences," I said to myself, "and they didn't affect me this much." But I just couldn't shake those feelings.

I attempted to channel the nervous energy. I began to make decisions about things that I'd been putting off for years. The hardest, for everyone, was the divorce. In addition, I began to search for some reason why I had kept so many emotions buried for such a long time. Of course, this didn't happen overnight. For some time, I'd been feeling the need to make a significant change in my life, but I didn't know how or where to start.

I started by looking at myself in the mirror and asking myself, truly, whether I was happy with my life. I found that I couldn't answer myself. I cleansed all my personal relationships of ambiguities, lies, and misunderstandings. Maybe that will all sound a bit too technical, but it's my way of explaining to you that I relieved myself of some of the baggage that had left both my feet and my spirit dragging.

Some people I thought were my friends remained stuck in the old ways. They had a specific, distorted image of me. But others opened their worlds to me and accepted me as I am. I also forced myself to go out more, to talk with people more, to say what was really on my mind, and I promised myself that I would no longer waste any time hiding myself behind façades.

It hasn't been easy.

There's nothing easy about remaking your life at the age of forty-nine, especially when it involves reacquainting myself with things that I had buried and left for dead long ago.

The strangest thing of all is that it wasn't my adventures as a war correspondent (which I'll write about in greater detail in another letter) that brought me to change my way of life. No. The change came about because of that one ominous morning when I was on my way to the dentist. There are no ceremonies or speeches at the moment of death. They might come later but never at the precise moment where life flickers and fades away.

I'd thought about the possibility of dying in Iraq or Afghanistan, en route to Kuwait or in the mountains of El Salvador, or flying across the border between Colombia and Venezuela. But never just a few miles from my home.

Soon I came to learn that those were the rules life plays by, and that—far from tormenting myself—I should take advantage of what I have, enjoy my time with you and with my friends and family to the fullest, and to be brutally honest with myself. You have to live life as it comes without trying to force it to fit certain preformed plans.

And that's the way I've tried to be ever since.

From that moment onward, I've had a mental clarity that had eluded me for years. I realized that life flies by us all, and it made me angry to think about all the many moments that I'd lost. I had to take more advantage of the time I have with you, and I had to open myself up emotionally to those around me. Hiding my feelings in the hopes of a more propitious time was just wasting time. In other words, there's no such thing as later.

> ~ **Hiding my feelings in the hopes of a more propitious time was just wasting time. In other words, there's no such thing as later.**

And I changed.

Before, I don't think I would have been able to write these letters to you. But now I write from a new place, both inside and out. I write from a desk facing a window that looks out over a lovely garden. I don't write facing the wall, like I did before. I write surrounded by natural light, without fears, and smiling.

And I started listening to music again in earnest. I never even realized how long it had been since I sought out music. I bought an iPod and started looking for songs like someone might seek water in a desert. The liberating power of music fascinated me. I started singing along, by myself, while running or driving, and I moved a mountain's worth of feelings through my mouth. I found music for the second time in my life—the first time was back when I was twelve years old and taking classical guitar lessons—and it was just as thrilling.

It's one thing to say that life is short, and it's something else entirely to absolutely believe that statement as truth. And when I saw death pass me by just a few inches beyond my driver's side window, things changed. I can tell you that today I am much hap-

THE GIFT OF TIME

A mother is a person who seeing there are only
four pieces of pie for five people, promptly
announces she never did care for pie.

—TENNEVA JORDAN

To my mother's grandchildren:

It was my mom, your grandma, who taught me that time is a
gift. By her own logic, she's practically Santa Claus. My mother
has given us almost all of her time, and she continues to do so. I
can't think of a better way of loving someone.

Remember the last trip we took with her to Colorado? As
soon as the two of you had gotten out of bed, she was already
there in the kitchen, ready with breakfast. Then we left her alone
for a few hours while we went off to ski (she preferred to skip
that part of the trip, due to the pain in her knees). But when we
returned, there she was: waiting to hear all about what we'd done
that day. The times when she wasn't there for us are few and far
between.

That's how my mom has been, ever since we were children.

At that age, I never understood the importance of and the

time required to be a good mother (or father). It's a full-time job, and that's something I couldn't fully appreciate until you both were born. But today I know more than ever just what my mother did for my siblings and me.

I don't know why the image I have of her—stretched out on her bed reading—is so etched into my mind. The lamp there on the little bedside nightstand is lit. Then I enter her room, she looks at me, closes her book without a second thought, and smiles.

The feeling that her time was mine has been with me forever. I can't remember a single moment when I needed to talk to her and she wasn't there for me.

～ **The feeling that her time was mine has been with me forever. I can't remember a single moment when I needed to talk to her and she wasn't there for me.**

When we were young, my siblings and I would come home from school around four in the afternoon, open the door, and yell, in unison, "Ma, we're home!" And, of course, she was there.

The few times when she wasn't always surprised us. "Where's Mom?" we asked our nanny, as if my mother didn't have the right to go out and do her own things, as if her only obligation was to take care of us. I always knew that she would be there whenever my siblings or I needed her.

Now that I think about it, it seems like a risky bet. She lost her own mother when she was very young, but—as a child—it never even crossed my mind that one day she wouldn't be with us. No. "That's not going to happen to my mom," I thought. Today, I want to keep thinking that way.

My mom made my three brothers, my sister, and me believe

that her primary mission in life—the only mission that mattered, really—was to spend time with us.

Time.

In the book *Shouts and Whispers*, the Mexican writer Elena Poniatowska found the perfect way to explain this obsession with time felt by those who have lost it: "Time, give them time (my children, my grandchildren, and my friends), make time for them out of my own life, for the only thing that I can offer them is my time, whatever time I have left to give. Perhaps I didn't give them enough of it during my career as a writer, especially since—to me—the most important thing of all is them, their wants and needs, their failures, their embarrassments, their joys, their life."

My mother took time out of her own life to give to us as well. But as a child, I couldn't appreciate it. Until now.

To a child, time isn't that important. It's what we have the most of. We are pure promise. At least that's what we think. And I spent the majority of my days playing, studying, and killing time. Then came the long days in the high school located over an hour from my house, and scrambling to finish my homework so I could go out and play in the street with my friends.

These days, instead of going out to play in the street, kids might go to the mall or play video games. But playing in the streets was the best. That's where life took place: Soccer was played, romances were kindled, fights broke out, friends were made, parties were planned, candy was bought and sold . . . it all happened on the street.

All the while, my mom was waiting at home.

When we finally got tired from all that playing (if that were even possible) and came in for a glass of water—or literally to stick my head in the refrigerator, breathless, in an attempt to cool off—there was *la Jechu*, as we always called her.

The boss lady. And sometimes she got angry. But even in those cases, we knew that the punishment would be fair. And she often seemed more uncomfortable than we did when she was doling out a well-deserved reprimand for some prank or mischief we'd pulled.

One time—just one time!—she went so far as to spank me for something awful I must have done, though I don't remember what it was. Still, however deserved it was, it must have upset her, because soon after she came to me and apologized. The lesson I learned from my mother's apology for giving me a well-deserved spanking is an enduring one. I knew that violence didn't teach positive lessons. Now, as a father myself, my intention was never to use such methods of discipline.

I know that there are other parents out there who believe in a spank or a smack as a means of discipline. But I soundly reject that philosophy. If we teach our children to use force whenever words or reason fail, we are promoting violence as a means of solving conflicts. That reminds me, at least, of war.

But *la Jechu* rarely punished us. She ran her household and raised her children with communication and a firm belief in the power of organization. I remember that sense of order to my mother's house—one that gave it a welcoming sense of security. Nothing could happen to us inside that home. Even after two burglaries—one of which was so brazen that the thieves opened some bottles of liquor and left a half-finished game of chess behind them—that house maintained its sense of inviolability.

Neither of the burglaries happened while we were home. Which is why my parents, despite their obvious nervousness, were able to convince us, still, that nothing bad would ever happen to us in that house. And that's how it was until we moved away. Every moment we felt safe. She gave us that gift.

If there is one thing that I've tried to take from my mom, it's the way she managed her time. I like making you feel that you can come to me at any time. But now that I'm a father, I've realized that something that seemed so natural—giving the gift of time—is one of the hardest things a family can do. How can I convince you that you can talk with me at any time, even when I'm thousands of miles away covering a story? How can I ever fill you with that same sense of absolute security that I got from my own mother if it requires a constant and assured presence?

~ **I like making you feel that you can come to me at any time. But now that I'm a father, I've realized that something that seemed so natural—giving the gift of time—is one of the hardest things a family can do.**

I'm sure you'd tell me that I shouldn't be so dramatic, that that's what cell phones and e-mail are for. True. But I'm convinced that there's something different about children who can hear their father's voice in person, as opposed to needing a digital connection. The difference is closeness, that is what I felt as a child from my mom. One of the moments that I enjoy most with you two is when you go to bed. Completely separate from the day's complications or our own moods, that's the moment when we can put everything aside and talk together.

Stroking your foreheads before saying goodnight and shutting off the light has become a marvelous and comforting experience for me. It is the single most peaceful moment I can imagine. When I watch you close your eyes, I can feel myself being transported to some other world, and that that softest of caresses has sent you into a deep sleep. "So much," I'll sometimes say to myself, knowing that—right there—I am the happiest dad in the world.

Though I have to admit, I learned that from my mother as well.

In a house with five children, there isn't much time for personal attention. Almost everything has to be done as a group effort or activity. Every night, before bedtime, my mom would give each of us a little stroke across the forehead. It lasted for only a moment: Mom had to make the full round of kids, and of course she was exhausted from the day's tasks. But those few seconds were, for me, the best ones of the day.

She was ever watchful and constantly supportive. Whether I was spending hours practicing to be a concert-level classical guitarist (something that I eventually abandoned because I didn't have a good ear, deciding instead to attend college) or whether I was dreaming of reaching the Olympics as a track-and-field athlete, my mom was always the first one to listen to a new song I'd learned or to congratulate me for dropping my time in the four hundred meters by a fraction of a second. However, the best example I have of her unconditional support happened when I was much younger.

For a while in Mexico, a popular toy was a wooden car about a meter long, which you could kneel on and push along the ground with one of your legs. They were quite fun. Also, they could accommodate a two-man crew, with one person steering while the other pushed from behind. Everyone on my block wanted one, but—of course—they were too expensive. My parents couldn't afford to buy one.

So it was that one day, out of pure frustration and determination, I decided that I was going to build my own wooden car. I collected some roller skates, tires from other cars, broomsticks, splintered lumber, and shoelaces of all colors, and set about assembling my little car with a hammer and nails. The end result looked like what it was—an assortment of junk—but surprisingly, it bore my weight and its wheels turned.

My mom, of course, saw cause to celebrate. She convinced me that I'd created a marvel of engineering, and—even though the rickety car lasted only a day—she made me feel like the proudest kid on earth. The same thing happened when I was six: I was trying to paint a horse using a very intricate "color by number" technique. I almost gave up right from the start.

"It's too hard, Mom," I said. "I can't paint a horse." But she insisted.

So I continued to work patiently at the easel for several nights before going to bed. And, much to my surprise, the image of a beautiful horse began to appear on the page. And my enthusiasm was growing along with it. A week later, when I finished the painting, I couldn't believe what I was looking at.

As you might imagine, my mother's reaction made me believe that someday—if I truly wanted to—I could become an artist. Again, an absolute exaggeration. But to this day I still look at that painting (now hanging in my office) and feel proud. That invaluable sense of security that my mother bestowed upon me when I was younger is still with me today. It's yet another of her many gifts. And an example of her sacrifice.

One afternoon, just as I was about to head out the door to go play in the street with my friends and brothers, my mom stopped me. I remember seeing her standing there, in the kitchen doorway, just off the garage.

She was smiling, but her eyes were weary. It was as if she had suddenly learned of something very important and needed to tell me before it burned her up inside. Without any lead-up or introduction, my mom asked me if I believed in happiness. That was it. At ten years of age, I figure that I was basically dumbstruck.

But this was my mother talking to me. And despite my passive and slightly surprised reaction, she went on:

"Happiness lies in the little moments," she said. "It's not permanent."

I'm convinced that that was the day that my mother left. That fine afternoon, she came to understand that the story she'd been raised with—that happiness lies in getting married and having a large family—was filled with holes. It was that precise moment where she finally dared to ask herself if she was truly unhappy as a woman.

True, she had a husband who provided for the family, five mischievous yet amiable children, and a home for them all to live in. And from time to time, that was enough to engender happiness. But something was missing. Something vital. From that point on, she went off in search of it, and I think that to this day, she's searching still.

Our travels together to China and India were powerful, almost spiritual experiences that brought us even closer. Traveling with either only your mother or your father is unlike anything else. It creates bonds of intimacy that are impossible to form under other circumstances.

Years later, when I was away at college, she decided to enroll herself in order to take a few classes on human development. I would pass her in the hallways, and I couldn't help but think that my mother was living a sort of delayed youth. That woman with five children, a husband, and barely a high school education was looking for something new, and she wasn't about to stop until she found it. She had rebelled against an unfulfilling life.

Eventually, my mom was daring to ask herself the questions that she'd kept buried for so many years. And here I am, surprised to be doing the same thing. It's just in our family's nature,

I guess. Today, I know that my mom is at peace. She's still taking classes—currently, they're music, philosophy, and the history of religion—and she smiles ear to ear whenever she realizes that her interests don't necessarily correspond to what you'd usually expect from a seventy-year-old woman. She taught me that happiness will bubble to the surface, and that when you're not completely happy with your life, you have to take bold steps to break out of the mold, because otherwise you can suffocate. It's a harsh but invaluable lesson to learn.

> She taught me that happiness will bubble to the surface, and that when you're not completely happy with your life, you have to take bold steps to break out of the mold, because otherwise you can suffocate.

"Tell us another true story!" That's what you said to your grandmother not too long ago, Nico.

And she sorted through her ample repertoire of family anecdotes for one that would perfectly fit the present occasion. This time it was a story about the pranks and antics your uncle Alejandro used to pull when he was your age. And you sat there, listening happily and barely even blinking. That's how it's always been.

My mom is the vault for family lore. She smoothly and subtly weaves the memories she gathers about all her children and grandchildren, dealing them out with generosity and care. It is all about making connections, not about embarrassment. You almost never hear anything in her family stories that would hurt someone's feelings. She knows that things said among family carry greater weight.

One poorly placed word can ruin a relationship for years.

An insult from a stranger might bother you, but if it comes from a sibling or other close family member, it can tear your life to pieces. My mom keeps track of everything, from who goes on a trip to who stays home and what they are doing there. She is also an infallible human birthday calendar. "Today is Ger's birthday," she warns. "Don't forget to call him."

Her specialties are the "true stories." They're the stories that have come to identify our family. They almost always produce curiosity and surprise. Like the day when my brother Eduardo broke his nose on a parked car's grille . . . while playing football. Or the aunt who could shrink her brain. Or the adventures of Uncle Armando, who once jumped off a trampoline into an empty pool.

Of course, she would always put her own personal spin on the "true stories," so that we could learn just a little bit more about her. It still pains me when she tells us about the day when her own mother died after a long battle with cancer; she was still a child, and in the confusion of the moment, nobody explained to her what had happened. That left a mark on her. For many years, she was an invisible child.

But it's not all tragedy. She also often recalls a long and happy trip to Spain that she took with her father, which went on for some weeks longer that expected, much to the surprise and consternation of my father. Those were her first small rebellions against the way of life that others had chosen for her.

The importance of the "true stories" was rooted not only in their essential content—for they had given continuity and context to our lives—but also in the way in which they taught me to tell stories. And I suppose that these letters to you are my own set of "true stories."

I've also tried to learn the particular way in which she could put herself in another person's shoes. History and storytelling are ultimately for the listener's benefit. Or are they? Not too long ago I received a phone call from my mom informing me that a very close friend of the family had passed away. But instead of delivering the news like a slap in the face, she first told me how she had recently visited our good friend's children. Only then did she open up and gently tell me the sad news about our friend. There was no doubt about it: Even though I was nearly fifty years old, she was still thinking of my feelings first. At that age, she was still taking care of me. And that disarmed me.

Once, when I was still a teenager, my mom suggested I read every letter to the editor and editorial column in the daily paper. "That's where you go to find out about all the important things going on in the world." The exercise wasn't an easy one. In the 1970s, the Mexican press was a very closely monitored, timid, and God-fearing industry. The letters and editorials in the *Excelsior*, which is what my parents read, were filled with secrets and cryptic phrases. You had to read between the lines if you wanted to understand what the journalist was really trying to say. Writing in a direct, critical style about authority wasn't the norm. But I learned to enjoy those editorials with their hidden messages, some of which bordered on the subversive while others weren't so.

Decades later, I had become the journalist writing his own opinions. And I've never forgotten the enormous power that a mother's simple suggestion can have on her son. "You don't have to be a politician in order to change the world," she said to me once. And I've tried to follow that advice faithfully.

From my mother, I learned to always listen before speaking, to understand the power of a cool hand upon the forehead, to tell "true stories," to read the editorial pages, to fight for what I want, and to admit that happiness comes at a moment's notice and then—*poof!*—it's gone. She is a tireless traveler—in fact, she recently called me to say that she was taking a solo trip through northern Spain—but, above all else, she is the best traveling companion that a boy could ever have wanted.

~ **From my mother, I learned to always listen before speaking, to understand the power of a cool hand upon the forehead, to tell "true stories," to read the editorial pages, to fight for what I want, and to admit that happiness comes at a moment's notice and then—*poof!*—it's gone.**

My mother is no feminist, but in her own way she forever changed her family and her children by having the courage and belief in herself to change her destiny. She started late, but she applied herself, and ever since her childbearing years were over, she got right into the rhythm of the world.

The best gift in the world is to give a bit of your time to others.

I love you in rivers,
Yuyú's oldest son

Letter 4

TO WITNESS A WAR

⌒

Only the dead have seen the end of the war.

—PLATO

To those whom I love the most:

Things are not necessarily as you expect them to be. The most delightful bathroom I've ever beheld was at the Singhar Hotel in Jalalabad, Afghanistan, in the middle of a war zone. This is the story of that trip, which was very nearly my last.

My journey to Afghanistan in December of 2001 was one of those predictable acts of hubris and stupidity that journalists commit when they can't resist the urge to witness firsthand what goes on in a time and place of great strife. At that time, Afghanistan was one of the most dangerous places in the world. The station had decided not to send anyone, a decision I disagreed with, though I understood their apprehension. I did the only thing I could—took some vacation time and endeavored without their support.

The hunt for Osama bin Laden was at its peak. His encampment was reported to be in an abandoned house next to the wreckage of a tank. That tank became a reference point for American viewers during the war. It was the same tank that I saw on TV on Thanksgiving Day when I decided to go to Afghanistan. I didn't tell you two beforehand. It's one of those things that don't usually come up as a light topic of conversation after a soccer match or a night at the movies.

It was the same tank that I saw on TV on Thanksgiving Day when I decided to go to Afghanistan. I didn't tell you two beforehand. It's one of those things that don't usually come up as a light topic of conversation after a soccer match or a night at the movies.

It's hard to explain to someone who isn't a journalist exactly what draws us into conflict zones. Reporters seek out parts of the world that other people try to avoid. What is even more absurd and incredible is that we enjoy it. There's nothing more frustrating to a newshound than being away from the action when our world is transforming.

This time was different. I regretted it upon the first moment I was forced across the Torkham border between Pakistan and Afghanistan. I was risking my life—and your futures—in a very foolish way. But what I remember with absolute clarity is that, after committing the grave error of taking a solo trip to the Afghanistan combat zone, it was the two of you who enabled me to keep my focus and my life intact. I never stopped thinking about the two of you. Strangely enough, I thought much more about you while I was in Afghanistan than when I'm in Miami.

"I have to get out of here; I have to see my kids," I was constantly saying. "I have to see them again."

I wanted to reach the mountains of Tora Bora, near Jalalabad, where the U.S. Army was searching for Osama bin Laden. At the time, the United States had the backing of a good part of the world. A few years later, everything would be different.

To reach Jalalabad, first you have to negotiate a winding, twisting Pakistani mountain road. I was moved to learn that I would be going through the narrow Khyber Pass, which Marco Polo had himself taken in 1275. In this ancient and beautiful place, I was reminded what that very same adventurous gentleman had to say of his journeys: "I have not told half of what I saw," and I became that much more determined to see you again, to tell you so much more than half of what I have seen—the good and the bad.

One month earlier, four journalists had been robbed and killed on an Afghan highway, and I was sincerely terrified at the idea of running into the same sort of luck. Credit cards didn't do much good in that part of Afghanistan.

Through my Pakistani guide, Naim, I paid one hundred dollars to hire three soldiers—who were under orders from the region's tribal chief, Haji Zaman—and we got in an old Toyota truck for the forty-nine-mile drive from the Afghanistan-Pakistan border to Jalalabad. Then things became interesting.

I was sitting in the middle of the backseat, with a soldier on each side of me. Kafir, some twenty-odd years in age, was playing with his Kalashnikov and—as the truck was bouncing along the decrepit road—he pointed it directly under my chin. It seemed to amuse him.

"What am I doing here?" I thought. "If something happens to me here, nobody is ever going to find out about it."

Things got much more complicated when—in a low voice and with a very rudimentary command of English—Kafir told me that he was a follower of bin Laden. My first reaction was to jump from the truck and hit the ground running, but I had two militants on either side of me and, even if I did manage to get out, I'd surely be stopped by a bullet in the back.

In reality, it was no surprise that Afghanistan contained members of Al-Qaeda and Taliban collaborators. A few weeks before my trip, this was the norm. After the first series of strikes by the U.S. military, things changed. But not too quickly. And what Kafir said to me was proof positive that those first few bombs hadn't necessarily changed any hearts or minds.

My stomach was tied up in knots. I had heard him clearly, and could feel him shifting in his seat. I was sweating profusely despite the wintry cold, and I decided to offer Kafir something that—I hoped—might save my skin.

I told him that if he took care of me, I would take care of him. I wouldn't let myself think about those four journalists who had been killed in November of 2001, and I felt in my own flesh the tenuous nature of life in Afghanistan in those days.

Kafir understood that my proposition meant money for him, and he lowered his rifle from beneath my chin. Apparently, this whole brief exchange happened without the knowledge of my guide or any of the other guards. But it seems to me that such a blatantly lethal game couldn't have taken place without the cooperation of the other passengers. Kafir stopped talking about Osama, and I remained silent for the rest of the drive.

Before the trip, a producer friend of mine (who'd helped me find a guide in Pakistan and put me in touch with the people from CNN in Afghanistan) gave me some valuable advice. "Don't carry a lot of big bills with you," she said. "It's much better to carry a big stack of ones." And despite the bulkiness, that's exactly what I did.

When I reached the hotel in Jalalabad where the international correspondents were staying, Kafir signaled to me with his rifle to get out of the truck and follow him. But I only dared to step a few feet away from the vehicle. I wasn't safe quite yet, but I felt more protected there, with the other journalists just inside the hotel.

I reached inside the little travel pouch that I was wearing next to my body and felt out fifteen dollar bills. I handed them to Kafir. Just fifteen dollars. He took them and looked them over with a certain curiosity. I wondered if he'd ever seen real one-dollar bills before. Then, without saying a thing, he looked away and fixed his eyes on the hotel entrance. I interpreted his gesture as permission to leave, and quickly got my bag and headed for the lobby. I didn't dare to look back.

My life in Afghanistan was only worth fifteen dollars.

Regret—for not weighing the risks of my trip more carefully beforehand, which in the previous few hours had been muscled aside by fear (the more persistent and stronger emotion)—welled up again. I felt like a fool, rather than the humanitarian journalist I imagined myself to be. Very few people knew that I was even going to Afghanistan, and even less knew how dangerous it was turning out to be. At best, it was a few pages in the autobiography I was working on, but it was an incredible gamble: Death or serious injuries aren't worth that. The hole I could leave in your lives wouldn't be worth that.

The empty space is the thing that hurts most when we lose a father. It's an absence impossible to fill. It's a phone call with nobody on the other end. I imagined the looks on your faces if you would ever have to explain to your friends that your dad had died in a war zone—that he had gone there of his own accord, dispatched by no one.

But there I was, and I decided to redefine my mission so that—more than simply being a journalist—I would be a survivor. To come out alive. That was all I wanted to do at that point. I had committed one error in embarking on the trip, but I wasn't about to commit a second.

Once I had reached Afghanistan and felt the fragility of human life there, I developed a plan for returning to Pakistan as soon as possible, and from there, the United States. But it took me several days to manage it.

I spent nights in Afghanistan in a state of near-constant watch. I slept without really sleeping, ever conscious of the slightest sounds of movement around me. My senses were heightened by the danger. I understood that my only job was to stay alive and get home to see you both again. Once again, kids, you were going to save me.

The days after my arrival dragged on and on. I linked up with a caravan of journalists working for CNN who were heading to Jalalabad through the mountains of Tora Bora, where some of the most intense fighting was taking place. On the way there, we saw extreme poverty, children with their faces looking out from mud and cardboard huts, in harsh and inhospitable landscapes that seemed to have come directly out of biblical times.

In that environment of almost-constant violence and fear, the most simple and trivial things took on a very new and distinct dimension. Those chocolate-flavored energy bars for which I had only a passing fondness were suddenly the most delicious treats imaginable, traded and shared during the course of the day as if currency. The Spanish correspondent who loaned me his satellite phone twice a day so I could call home and let everyone know I was all right felt like a brother to me. And the chats I had with the CNN reporter, Brianne Leary, were filled with humor and optimism even during the most tense moments we faced, and always helped to distract me and to focus my thoughts on things far away from death. (Brianne, who lives in New York, still sends me beautiful Christmas cards designed with an Afghan motif every year. The proceeds from the sale of these cards go directly to a group that supports Afghani women.)

After that experience, I've tried to appreciate and be thankful for all things, no matter how small. And I think I've come home from that experience a more prudent man, someone who is less preoccupied with material goods. It was a small thing to take away.

Speaking of small things, who would have ever thought that I would take the best shower of my life in that place? I'd decided not to risk anything else by returning to the combat zone. So that December morning, with the desert sun shining, I stayed behind in the hotel while other correspondents were leaving for the mountains of Tora Bora.

I had become optimistic; I had worked out a way to return to Pakistan with a group of journalists the following day. I didn't want to repeat the terrible experience of my arrival.

It had been five or six days, and I still hadn't taken a bath, and I didn't think that I would be able to until I'd left Jalalabad. But another journalist confided to me—sotto voce—that on the second floor of the hotel there was a shower. With hot water. I selected the least dirty clothing that I had left and went out in search of that alleged shower.

Upon finding it, I turned one of the faucets and out came a marvelous, steaming cascade of hot water. I couldn't believe it. I quickly removed my clothes and slipped into the water. *Ahhh.* The rest of the bathroom (it must be said) was disgusting. But that little space in which I washed was like my own personal paradise. One of the windows in the bathroom was broken, and I could see the mountains surrounding the city. The sound of running water muffled the distant drones of the B-52 bombers flying high above.

I stood there, motionless, my hands held to my chest, for ten or fifteen minutes. I felt all of my fears being washed away down the drain with the water. There, for a moment, I didn't need anything else. When the water began to run cold—I had probably used all the hot water in the whole hotel—I shut off the faucet and used a dirty white shirt as a towel.

"It's time to go home," I said to myself with absolute conviction as I dried off my hair.

War is failure.

War is the absolute confirmation that we fail as human beings, that we cannot converse with one another, that we aren't as ready as we think we are, that we haven't learned from the fighting—and the dying—that came before us.

War is nonsense, my children. Literally nonsense.

I have found myself in five war zones—El Salvador, Kosovo, the Persian Gulf, Afghanistan, and Iraq—and let me say this: I have never seen a good war, a noble war.

One of the things that impressed me most about every battlefield is the isolation of the combatants—they have the tunnel vision of a rifle barrel. The external world disappears, and the only thing that matters is putting an end to the enemy. All possible arguments boil down to one single essential: Kill that which seeks to kill me.

War forces soldiers, guerrillas, militiamen, and terrorists alike to erase everything before and after. Kill or be killed. The person standing in front of you is not a father, not a son, not a friend of anybody. War strips you of your environment because—if it doesn't—you can't kill. How could you shoot someone if you're worried about whether he has any children? How can you kill a young man if you're thinking about the grief of his parents?

Nothing is more dangerous than dividing the world into black and white, into good and evil. Rulers who think in such terms are like cowboys in a power struggle. Even the dumbest of them feel superior to the others. And that always results in confrontation.

That is why wars motivated by religion are so bloody and inhuman: Your very salvation depends on the destruction of your enemy. Killing in the name of a god or by divine order is a vile contradiction.

There's a strange sense of inevitability in war. The sort that won't stop until the other side disappears.

One of war's greatest injustices is that those doing the fighting are, generally, not the same people who are giving the orders to fight. If all presidents who initiate a war were required to have children on the front lines, how many wars would there be?

⌣ One of war's greatest injustices is that those doing the fighting are, generally, not the same people who are giving the orders to fight. If all presidents who initiate a war were required to have children on the front lines, how many wars would there be?

I remember when I learned this.

It was the mid-1980s, and I was climbing the mountains surrounding San Salvador, on my way to interview the guerrillas fighting the right-wing government. We were on our way to see

37

the *muchachos*, which is what they called the poor farmers in the region who supported and protected the guerillas. The problem is that they *were* muchachos—just boys. These were not men with the weight of wisdom and experience on their side. They were children, twelve or thirteen years old. They underwent their military training with a serenity that bordered on the ridiculous. They were being taught to kill. And, as you've certainly taught me, there's nothing more serious than a focused, resolute teenager or child.

The very idea that either of you would go running off into the mountains with a rifle in your hands is unthinkable. But for many young boys and girls, that is their daily reality. The thin, camouflaged bodies of these children would hide among the mountain forests as military helicopters passed overhead. I remember standing in awe, frustration, and fear beneath the pounding of the rotors.

"One false move," I thought, "and they'll fill us with holes."

But the children didn't move; they had melded into the mountain.

The image of those child warriors was one of the most startling and gruesome I'd seen. There's just nothing more unbearable than the spectacle of a child ready to die for a cause he or she doesn't even understand. But hardly anyone saw them there in the mountains as I did, and the war raged on. Tens of thousands died, and nobody knew what had happened to them.

It was during that war in El Salvador when I first prayed for my life. And it was the last time, too.

Sometimes, when I was a boy, I would pray before going to bed. But I did it mechanically, like a lullaby to myself. In primary school, at Mass every Friday, I prayed then, too. I had to. But when I was older and no longer obligated to pray, I stopped.

I know that the two of you will sometimes pray, and I think this is a good thing. Everyone should take hold of support whenever they can, and the meditative beauty of praying can be a wonderfully restorative thing. If praying brings you inner peace or a sense of tranquility, I hope you always keep it with you. However, I do hope you never pray the way I did when I was a boy: out of obligation and fear.

But that day I prayed.

It was election Sunday in early 1989, and as we were driving down the street we suddenly found ourselves caught in a crossfire between a military force and the guerrillas. I ran out of the van along with the producer and the cameraman, and hid out in a shack.

It wasn't good.

The army helicopters probably confused us with the guerrillas (who dressed in civilian clothes) and began to fire on us from the sky with their machine guns. The bullets were flying right by us, and the shell casings were raining down and bouncing off the corrugated zinc roof. I panicked.

Now, kids, this might seem ridiculous to you—I have no idea why it crossed my mind at that moment—but it seemed too early to die. Not too early in my life—just too early in the *morning*. It wasn't yet seven.

I curled up as small as I could against one wall of that humble little house sheltering us and began to pray. And it wasn't an Our Father or a Hail Mary. It was something more of a plea to God to perhaps not kill me right then. Probably worthless. After all, how could a few words stop a hailstorm of bullets? Nevertheless, I continued. The repetition, the way it forced me to breathe, calmed me down somewhat.

It was twenty minutes of horror. For the first time, I felt that animalistic fear of being on the verge of death. My stomach was queasy and my hands and feet were shaking, and my teeth were chattering so violently that I couldn't even speak. I had wanted to be a war correspondent for years, but when it came time for my debut, I nearly choked.

Later, I felt like a hypocrite. I've never been a religious person, and clearly I had been praying out of desperation. I wasn't convinced, either by what I was saying or what I was asking for. It was like being back in primary school, where I would repeat the words without really understanding them. The awful sensation of losing control in the face of fear bothered me as much as the fact that I broke down to pray in what I thought might be my final moment. The fraud made me sick to my stomach.

I don't believe that human beings have a destiny. Nor do I believe that someone or some thing can decide when and how we will die. I don't believe in any of that, and I don't believe in miracles, either.

Life and death are uncertain and random. Circumstantial. A spermatozoan—one of millions—unites with an ovum; one bullet misses by a millimeter. Life and death depend on these things.

When I returned to the hotel that afternoon, I learned that on that same day, three journalists had been killed. I was saved.

The theme of war and its apparent inevitability has always fascinated me. Reading about it helps me to come to terms with it, though no explanation, even those by the greatest thinkers, has ever satisfied me.

In a 1932 letter he wrote to Sigmund Freud, Albert Einstein asks a key question: "Is it possible to free mankind from the unfortunate fatality of war?"

Freud, searching for answers, replied that "wars will only be prevented with certainty if mankind unites in setting up a central authority to which the right of giving judgment upon all conflicts of interest shall be handed over." Freud wrote that thirteen years after the creation of the League of Nations and thirteen years before the founding of the United Nations, neither of which has been able to prevent war from breaking out.

That ends the first argument.

My heart is heavy as I come to realize that with regard to war, your life is going to be much more difficult than mine was. Can we stop wars from happening? Freud told Einstein that, in order to prevent them, it's necessary to have a "cultural attitude and the justified dread of the consequences of a future war." And that requires our full attention and a productive conversation, don't you think?

There are entire societies that have taken on this pacifist principle. But it has to be accompanied by an appropriately fitting way of life: one without domestic abuse, corporal punishment of children (for a slap or a spanking are forms of intrafamily battles), access to video games that award points to whomever can decapitate the digital enemy, the overzealous hoarding and using of firearms, the sense of domination that comes from hunting, and without the shouts and insults that kill one's self-esteem.

War—and peace—are learned at home.

This is why I have never dared to move in violence against my children—not even a spank. No matter how poorly you might behave, it's not worth a blow. Plenty of parents who believe in corporal punishment have children who grow up fine, but it's very easy to cross the line into the realm of physical and psychological damage that will have lasting repercussions. Too many learn from their parents and other family members that violence is a legitimate method of solving conflicts. For them, war isn't a last resort, it's simply a way of being.

An antiwar cultural attitude can only be learned in the home and in a society that reinforces the values of negotiation and dialogue over confrontation and intolerance.

And ending a war involves exactly that: speaking with the enemy. Something that can seem inconceivable to the combatants. Dialogue is always war's first victim.

But even if we don't instill an antiwar attitude for the better, at least we can create a healthy fear—a terror—for wars. In fact, I disagree strongly with the censoring of war images on TV.

Many armies have policies that prevent the bodies of their fallen soldiers from being filmed or photographed. The rule has two purposes: to avoid adding to the pain of the soldier's family members, and to avoid eroding public support for the war and the morale of the troops.

Nevertheless, I believe that if—during a war—we were to see the bodies of our soldiers being shipped home, it would exert an enormous amount of pressure on our elected officials, forcing them to seek a diplomatic, nonmilitary solution. This is particularly true in the United States. Ever since the Persian Gulf War, we've become accustomed to seeing antiseptic "surgical strikes," filmed from the skies, which prevent us from ever seeing the true, bloody consequences of the bombings. The images of the aerial attacks in Kuwait, Afghanistan, and Iraq more closely resemble the screen shots from some highly sophisticated video game.

I'm certain that if the Americans and the British had seen TV coverage of the bodies of their troops or the tens of thousands of dead Iraqi civilians (who, according to the UN, often died needlessly), that war would have taken a different course. Quickly.

Not all the dead are equal. I saw, laid out on metal slabs in a Kuwaiti morgue, the perfectly aligned, refrigerated bodies of Kuwaiti citizens who had died during the 1990 Iraqi invasion. They were treated as first-class casualties. Off to the side, the bodies of Iraqi soldiers who had been killed during the invasion of Kuwait were piled up, an arm protruding here, a leg hanging there. They had been left to rot. The smell was so strong and sickening that it permeated my clothing. I threw it all away before I returned to the hotel.

A few days before the Americans arrived in Kuwait, the panorama was exactly the opposite. The dead Iraqis were being preserved while the Kuwaiti bodies had been tossed into a corner. Even in death, everything depends on circumstance.

War is a brutal thing. Therefore, the coverage of a war must be brutal as well. It *should* make whoever sees it sick to their stomach. It *should* put knots in your gut, force you to turn off the TV, and give you the worst nightmares. It should disturb you to the point where you simply cry out, "Enough already!"

If either of you does go on to become a journalist, I want you to remember that.

As Freud wrote, "the justified dread of the consequences of a future war" is something that anybody who works in the media business has an obligation to disseminate. It is the great irony: Covering war in its full dimension—and not in the sterilized, dehumanized manner that political leaders would want—is the way in which we journalists can contribute to a demilitarized future.

I would be lying if I said that there weren't any good moments during my time as a war correspondent. And it reminds me of something that Nora Ephron wrote back in 1973; namely that "the awful truth is that for correspondents war is not hell. It is fun."

Well, I might not go that far. Covering a war, my children, is never something fun. The constant presence of death prevents that. But a bullet whistling past you or bombs falling in the distance do have that way of fixing you to the moment. The survival instinct sets your heart racing. Adrenaline chases any thoughts of sleep or rest. You see and hear everything with heightened clarity. War drugs you, puts you in a state of hypersensibility. And that, to be honest, generates a certain sense of pleasure.

During my brief stay in Afghanistan, I spent a full week when I barely slept at all, and I don't remember ever feeling tired. That's not normal.

H. D. S. Greenway, himself a veteran of many wars, asks the following: "Why do journalists seek out wars? Is it for the glamour, the adventure, the adrenaline? Is it the desire to be in the front-row seat of history? Is it public duty, professional advancement?" And his answer is as simple as it is convincing: "All of the above . . ."

Why go to war? Because that is where you can find the best and the worst of humanity. Because there I have found ways to test myself. Because there I was able to find my own true limits.

Plus, I just can't shake it. It's my job and my passion. I need to see war in order to tell about it. And I've met some of my best friends in it. The solidarity that is formed during the most dramatic and intense of times is without parallel. It's one of the few good things about wars. I have dinner almost every Friday with two of my best friends—our bond forged in that situation. We laugh a lot, reminiscing over the days we spent together during the early stages of the war in Iraq, back in March of 2003. In some way, only the men I was honored to go into Iraq with can fully understand what it was like to live through those difficult days. Without any form of protection, and following a convoy delivering food to Iraqi civilians, we pushed from Kuwait into the border town of Safwan. We spent a good while walking through the streets of that poor village, interviewing Iraqis and watching the American tanks rolling deeper into their country.

In retrospect, it was madness. Soldiers and other followers of Saddam Hussein were almost certainly mixed in with the civilian population, and we were likely running the risk of taking a bullet from one of them. Or a mob could have overrun our truck and relieve us of our expensive camera gear. But neither one of those things happened.

Our Kuwaiti translator refused to enter Safwan with us, so the crew and I were on our own. Many correspondents were embedded with various American military units, while others bravely set up in Baghdad, which had yet to be liberated. But we wanted to be the first journalists to independently enter Iraq so that we could cover the arrival of the American military machine from inside Iraqi borders. And, despite the risk, we managed to do so.

What we reported that day—that American soldiers were not greeted with flowers and music but rather a good deal of hostility—was a clear signal of what was to come. And nobody can take that little bit of journalistic truth away from us. Was it worth the risk? That's impossible to know.

If one of us had been hurt or killed, the answer would be an unequivocal no. We would have been able to say that nothing is worth the death of a journalist. No piece of news is worth the loss of life. But since everyone came out unscathed, the shared experience and fear united the three of us.

Days after our incursion into Iraq, a missile hit a commercial center in the Kuwaiti city where we had been just two hours earlier. Though no one was killed, the explosion took place right next to where we had just had burgers and ice cream.

Back in the hotel, we passed around a bottle of whiskey (which I've never liked) to calm our nerves. There's nothing like facing up to your own mortality while in a circle of friends. It's something I'll never forget. We took care of one another during that war like family. The friendships you forge in wartime—and in other extremely stressful and difficult times—are, I believe, some of the finest in life.

Back at home, no matter how hard we tried to explain the details and intricacies of what we experienced in Iraq and Kuwait, only the three of us could fully comprehend it. Which is why I have dinner with my friends almost every Friday.

Jehona Aliu reminds me a lot of you, Paoli.

She is a five-year-old Kosovar-Albanian child whom I met in a refugee camp in Macedonia. Her story is a terrible one.

One night, Serbian soldiers entered Jehona's house in Urosevac, Kosovo, and forced her entire family to leave. Serbia's policy of ethnic cleansing left them with no recourse, and the Aliu family was forced to seek help near the Macedonian border. At the very least, they were able to get out alive.

They reached a temporary refugee camp, but in the chaos that was the norm in those days, the Macedonian government soon moved them to another camp, this one run by NATO, and it was there that Jehona went missing. She was one of over a thousand lost children who the Red Cross and UNICEF were trying to reunite with their families in that region of Macedonia.

I met her while she was playing in the mud next to the tent where she slept. For some reason (which I'm still not sure I understand), her coffee-colored eyes met mine, and a connection was formed. Perhaps it was because I saw something of you in her, Paola.

We couldn't communicate very well. She spoke Albanian, someone else translated it into Macedonian, my own translator rendered it into English, and I jotted it down in my notebook in Spanish. But despite the language barriers, we spent a good bit of time together.

I was moved by her vulnerability. I felt a lump rising in my throat. Her eyes said that she was alone in the world and that she couldn't go on like that, that she needed to find her family, that she couldn't understand why on earth this situation had befallen her.

What greater proof is there that the world is an unfair place?

Her hair was short, her features were fine, and she even forced a tenuous smile. Kosovar-Albanian children spend the day drawing houses. Burning houses. Houses riddled by bullets. Houses with shattered windows. Houses with knocked-down doors. Houses. The houses that they left behind, and the houses that are here—in the freezing mud of the refugee camp—they now long for.

Drawing houses is a therapy that, disguised as a game, gives the children something to do. "How else do they express the war trauma that they carry inside of them?" I asked one of the Stenkovec refugee camp directors. "It's simple," he said. "They touch you."

That was for sure. Those children who had never met me, who greeted me with *"Helou! Helou!"* would run right up to me for a hug or a pat on the back.

Like Jehona, Ardiana, a six-year-old girl, confronted me, her little hands propped up on her little hips, smiling disarmingly. I didn't share a word with her as there was no way for us to understand each other. But she never stopped smiling. How could she manage it? She'd lost everything, and yet there she was, smiling away. She had an internal strength that surprised me, and that I've yet to understand.

I think I see something of my children in every child I met from Kosovo. You were still so small, Nico, but I can't imagine you going through a life like the ones being lived by those refugee children. I dedicated myself to raising as much awareness as I could about the struggles—and the faces—of those children I met in Macedonia. It was the least I could do for them.

When I returned home from that trip, I hugged you both with all my strength. I'd like to think that you missed me during the two weeks that I was gone. But you could never imagine the terrible place that I went, and the extraordinary joy that it gave me to see you again. That contrast left me all but speechless for days afterward.

You were both so young, and I didn't tell you about it. Until now.

Have you noticed that soldiers almost never laugh or celebrate when they return home from war? Their families are the ones jumping for joy, but not them. Watch closely the next time you see a homecoming on TV.

The writer Walter Benjamin, whose books I read a lot in college, said that "silent soldiers, crippled, shell-shocked, return from the front to another no man's land." I would add that journalists do so as well. Wars create an armor plating around the heart. It doesn't matter if you're a soldier, a journalist, a medic, an observer, or a civilian. You cover your feelings.

Wars kill you from within. Psychologists call it post-traumatic stress disorder. You live in an anguished, mediocre center. You live in neutral. You've lived so much—and experienced such extremes—that your body, in order to protect itself, closes off from the exterior world.

Your interior reality—your memories, your nightmares, the images etched into your mind—dominate your external life.

Everything looks unreal, as if you're watching your life play out on a screen. Sometimes, other extreme sensations can temporarily return you to the here and now, but you quickly return to the daily tedium of not feeling anything.

I had begun to notice something during a surprising trip to India. The extreme poverty I saw in that country disturbed me deeply. And then, after experiencing the war in Kosovo, I found myself unable to talk about what I'd seen. It was as if I had become frozen from the inside.

After traveling to Afghanistan, the issue became much more serious. After days and weeks of friends and family asking me what was going on—and my guttural or monosyllabic responses of "fine," "more or less," or simply "grrr"—they stopped asking. Naturally. I don't even know how they endured that long.

I was acting more and more solitary. My conversations with other people were done in a cloud. I could hear the words, but they didn't mean anything; they were just a simple background hum. Everything was noise.

My good friend Gustavo, who has covered the most violent wars, has told me (over a marvelous dinner of grilled Argentine steak) about how he managed to keep the lines of communication open with other correspondents who—like him—have seen and suffered through the fall of Baghdad.

They talk about the things they can't share with their families. They share their fears. And that has saved them. But not everyone has a Gustavo to confide in. Too late, I realized that I was blocked up and growing ever more isolated. Years passed before I realized that I had shut myself off. So many wars, so many catastrophes, so many breaking stories, and so many unresolved, conflicted emotions, and I was simply passing the buck. Until I broke free.

And as I told you in an earlier letter, it wasn't a war that forced me to confront my emotional stubbornness and terrible existential anguish but a simple highway incident. You never know what the breaking point is when you've spent years hiding away your thoughts and feelings.

I still continue to work through that emotional frigidity. I feel like a sculptor chiseling away, piece by piece, at a mask that took years to set into place. And every time a piece of the shell falls away, I still feel the temptation to pick it up and put it back in its original place. I'm writing these letters to you so that you can truly know who is behind the mask. And it is, I think, a lifelong task.

I want always to feel like I did that one day when I arrived at JFK Airport in New York after covering the Persian Gulf War. I headed for the street, stepped on the sensor mat that automatically opened the wide glass doors, and I felt the marvelous gust of cold air hit my face. At that precise instant, I closed my eyes, let the sun warm my face, and—out loud—thanked the day that I was alive.

I love you both so much,
Papá (who went off to war and
came back to tell you about it)

THE SIMPLE PLEASURES OF A LIFE WITHOUT SMELL

~

Nothing revives the past so completely as a smell
that was once associated with it.

—VLADIMIR NABOKOV

To my children with beautiful, straight noses:

My nose doesn't work very well. It's the part of my body that
has taken the most punishment over the years . . . too much punishment, actually. If I could—if it wouldn't leave an awful, gap-
ing hole in the middle of my face—I would take it off at night
because during the day it's an inconvenient nuisance.

Over the years, my poor nose has been reduced to a flap of skin
hanging over a couple of bones, fractured beyond repair, and func-
tionally useless for years. And I'm stuck with it. Since, of course,
you see it all the time, you're used to its curves, points, and gouges.
I'm frequently amazed they let that mangled thing on television.

~ I'm frequently amazed they let that mangled thing on television.

I've never known this nose in a useful form. The doctor who delivered me used forceps—those awful baby tweezers by which some of us were yanked into this world. The problem is that the doctor, rushing through the procedure, caught my infant self by the *nose* with the forceps and, rather unceremoniously, jerked and tugged until the rest of me finally emerged from my mother's womb. *Crack.*

My mother remembers—with a bit of sadness and pain, as if it were her fault—that the first time she saw me I had an enormous red gash on my face, right across the bridge of my nose. I must have looked something awful because some of my mother's family pitied her with statements like "Poor thing, such an ugly little boy."

I never had the chance to thank the doctor for his fine, cautious, and professional use of the forceps, but that early event in my life would come to indelibly mark everything that would come later.

In 1926, in his final work titled *One, None, and a Hundred Thousand*, Luigi Pirandello wrote, "This nose hangs to the right." I like that book immensely, as the Italian writer describes a man who falls into an identity crisis after his wife innocently comments on a slight imperfection in his nose. He begins to obsess: Who am I? Am I the person I think I am, or am I the one seen by a hundred thousand others?

My nose also hangs to the right. And, just like Pirandello, ever since I was a child, I would stand in front of the mirror and push against my nose with all my strength in the hopes that eventually I would look less malformed. And I suppose that that trauma might also be the reason I usually sleep with the right half of my face on the pillow. I wanted to do whatever it took to straighten my nose.

That wasn't the only problem. My nose had a long, thin arc to it, which made me look like someone who might be a perfect case study for aspiring rhinoplasty performers. "How can this child breathe?" the students would wonder. And the answer was obvious: not well. Not well at all.

The curvature of my nose left one airway extremely narrow, while the other was left abnormally wide. And I wouldn't doubt that my right lung is noticeably larger than my left lung is.

Of course, none of this helped during the asthma attacks that I suffered as a child. In those days, we didn't have all the inhalers and other medical treatments that exist today, so often I would end up standing on tiptoe at the bathroom sink while my mother helped me breathe in the steam coming off the hot water.

Few human beings can say, the way I can, that the first moments of their lives were life-defining. I've had others, of course, but none of them have had such a significant influence on my day-to-day existence.

I'm talking about a life without smell.

I'm not like Grenouille, the marvelous—and terrifying—character in Patrick Suskind's novel *Perfume* who was born with no odor of his own. My body does indeed emit smells (let's call them "natural" smells) that any regular guy would usually prefer to conceal.

My problem is that I am almost completely unable to smell the world around me.

You heard it right. I can go to a restaurant and—if you were to blindfold me—you could pass dish after dish under my nose, and I would never know if it were beef, chicken, or fish . . . to say nothing of identifying the sauce it was served with. The most potent and sensual of perfumes pass unknowingly by me at parties and even when I greet someone with a kiss. And the breeze coming off the Dead Sea smelled the same to me as did the Pacific, the Mediterranean, and the Caribbean. Its high salt content and particular chemical makeup merely tickled my nose, the way all oceans do.

Though it may seem a curse, I recognize that this does come with certain benefits. Public bathrooms don't bother me, and I can emerge from airplane restrooms without a tortured look on my face. (Of course, I always wonder whether the next person to use the facilities after me might blame me for any lingering odors left from the visitor before me.) I am not disturbed by old shoes or wafting aromas of Roquefort cheese. I don't mind being surrounded by the other sweaty members of my yoga classes. I admit that I can even withstand the subways of the world—particularly the one in Moscow—without getting nauseated, even in the middle of summer. The scent of garlic and onion is simply a slight warmth on the breath of my dining companions. I can't tell the difference between someone with a bad case of halitosis and someone who brushes and flosses three times a day.

Though it may seem a curse, I recognize that this does come with certain benefits. Public bathrooms don't bother me, and I can emerge from airplane restrooms without a tortured look on my face.

I can handle the occasional flatulence with heroism, even if it's delivered with the volume of a military brass band inside a car with closed windows. Other, more solid emissions from a sick friend or family member are unpleasant, of course, to witness, but I have no problem consoling—from a certain distance—the person in distress. I score points that way.

So there are a few benefits to a life without smell, though of course the pleasure is mine. To put it simply and without any false modesty, I am a good travel and life companion. And I owe a great deal of that to my bum nose.

Despite all the aforementioned advantages, I live with the constant fear of not detecting my own offensive smells. I'm always the last to know if I smell bad. I shower constantly, both for hygiene and out of habit, although I can never tell if it's always necessary. It's by choice: I'm in a constant struggle to be the first to detect the smells I'm emitting. The insecurity makes me do it . . . either that or I just enjoy shelling out more money for soap and toothpaste than I should.

There's also the fact that I snore like a bull. How do bulls snore, you might ask? I just know that if someone has the misfortune of sharing my bed, they'll have to kick me at least a couple of times to get me to roll onto my stomach. Sleeping on my back is a dangerous thing.

But what can I say? My nose lives dangerously.

It has survived—at great cost—three frightening collisions. The first time was the forceps, which mashed it up good and proper. As a child, I didn't like my physical appearance. Still, though, there were more important things in life, like being able to go out and play in the street instead of being laid up in bed with an asthma attack.

With time, this changed. As a self-conscious teenager, appearance moved from annoyance to obsession. I wanted a new nose. There are ways of disguising big ears, ugly teeth, or even a lazy eye. But how do you hide a nose? Parties and gatherings of friends were always easier for me if they took place at night or when the lights were low.

I consulted several plastic surgeons, and each one told me the same thing: that I'd have to wait until I was seventeen or eighteen years old, when I was done growing. They didn't want to operate on a nose that would be growing again in just a few months. So I waited, waited, and waited impatiently . . . until one doctor performed a miracle.

The operation literally knocked me out. The discomfort of spending an entire week without being able to breathe through my nose was eclipsed by the hopes of seeing myself with a straight nose for the very first time. So when the doctor removed the bandages and I could finally look into a mirror, I almost didn't recognize myself. I had deep purple and green bruises around my eyes, and the skin on my cheeks had turned a shade between pale and paler. But none of that mattered, because right there, in the middle of my face, was a perfectly straight, functioning nose.

The operation was so successful that after a few months I forgot that I even had a nose. I'd never before gone a day without obsessing over it. For the first time in my life, I was—how can I put this?—de-nosified.

The joy of having a smooth, straight, functioning nose would not last long.

About a year after the surgery, I was playing in a high school basketball game. The game ended in a brawl, and the referee—who happened to be an alum of the opposing school—hit me from behind, his right fist landing squarely on my new nose. *Crack crack.* I knew what that sound meant: my second broken nose.

After the initial inflammation subsided, I was left with some serious deformities. And no matter how much I stood in front of the bathroom mirror trying to reset the fracture, it was to no avail. So that's how I spent the next two years until I was able to convince my father to pay for yet another surgery.

But this time, it wasn't so easy. The doctor warned me that the bones in my nose had taken so much abuse that there was no guarantee that another operation would be able to set it straight. Even so, I was willing to risk it. And what a risk it was!

The next one took place in the middle of a World Cup soccer summer, and the doctor and his assistants couldn't resist the temptation to bring a TV into the operating room so that they could watch the day's match. The anesthesiologist—in his passion for the game (I hope it's that, and not negligence)—didn't give me a high enough dose, and I woke up in the middle of the surgery. I remember it like it was yesterday: opening my eyes to find everyone else in the room staring at the TV screen. My nose wasn't their goal.

The doctor was stunned to see me awake and instantly ordered the anesthesiologist to immediately put me back under. I woke up hours later with the nagging feeling that all was not well. What had happened was that, after the anesthesia wore off, I had tried to pull off the bandages from my face. It took several doctors to subdue me.

Of course, my first conscious thought was "Who won the game?"

The third injury happened in the United States. My passion for soccer was greater than the warnings from my doctors that my nose wouldn't withstand another such blow. It was held together with tiny wires. But naturally, I paid them no heed.

While playing a pickup match, I tripped on the turf and—in a spectacular coincidence—my nose collided with a teammate's shoulder. *Crack crack crack.* The ball bounced away. I got up, gingerly touching my nose, certain that I was about to find myself on yet another operating table. But the game was still going on, and an opponent—chasing after the loose ball—ran straight into me. So that's how what was left of my nose was broken and rebroken for a third time.

A doctor in Los Angeles agreed to perform the surgery this time. However, after two previous, similar operations, the look of concern on his face was obvious. The existing damage had made it impossible to straighten it out fully this time. The medical concern was that the remaining bone tissue would be so brittle that the slightest touch would leave me with a deformed flap of skin in the middle of my face instead of a nose. The operation was as successful as could be expected. After all, my nose is something of a battlefield map. Any close examination reveals scars, bruises, irregularities, dents, and ridges. I have the nose of a boxer who's lost every fight by total knockout.

~ **Any close examination reveals scars, bruises, irregularities, dents, and ridges. I have the nose of a boxer who's lost every fight by total knockout.**

It defies all description. It's not a schnoz, it's more of a snake-shaped organ where mucus hides out in tiny passageways. Air struggles to flow through it, doing so in a hissing or, rather, a howling manner. And it hurts. It barely works at all, which is why I sometimes like shutting it down and only breathing through my mouth.

If I were to choose a personal deity, I would choose Yacatecuhtli, the god with the most famous nose in Aztec mythology. He was the venerated god of travelers and merchants. Reports given by the Spanish conquistadors describe him as having a long nose and carrying a staff. Now here's a god I can follow: a traveler with a big nose.

Yacatecuhtli, at least, could distinguish smells. My sense of smell, on the other hand, has atrophied for decades now, and is as good as dead.

The magic of visiting a place and recognizing it by its smell is foreign to me. I have no idea what that first sense of identification is like for normal people who perceive places by their scent. My world is olfactorally neutral. And that allows me to give a second chance to some places that others might reject out of hand. The sacred yet filthy Ganges River—one of the most heavily polluted rivers on earth—was, for me, a truly extraordinary experience. Despite the powerful stench of garbage, excrement, and dead bodies being burned in the open, I spent a majestic dawn on its banks. It was the view of the religious ceremonies being performed in the orange and bluish sunrise—and not the smells of putrefaction—that dominate my memories.

> **My world is olfactorally neutral. And that allows me to give a second chance to some places that others might reject out of hand. The sacred yet filthy Ganges River—one of the most heavily polluted rivers on earth—was, for me, a truly extraordinary experience.**

I have to open my eyes wide in order to know where I am.

And the fact that I can smell so few things has brought about my fascination with the olfactory system.

So it's no coincidence, then, that I share two of Marcel Proust's obsessions: time and smells. Marcel Proust, in writing *In Search of Lost Time*, tried—as I am trying with these letters—to recover lost moments, and his search began with the nose. There are countless anecdotes about the powerful effects of those fluffy French desserts known as *madeleines* ("An exquisite pleasure had invaded my senses," he writes) that take him back to his childhood. Such invisible sensual experiences are out of my realm of understanding.

Along with Proust and Suskind (whose character murdered

virgins in eighteenth-century Paris in order to harvest from them their unique scent), I understood early on what a pair of American doctors would discover much later. Richard Axel and Linda Buck won the 2004 Nobel Prize for Medicine for studying the processes by which the brain identifies smells. As you might imagine, kids, this subject is of no small personal importance. I want to know how you and the rest of the mortal world can smell things that I cannot.

After so many operations, I'm sure that I've destroyed many of the five million smell receptors located in the upper part of the nasal cavity that—in a normal person unlike me—enable you to distinguish some ten thousand different odors.

Ten thousand different smells! Who can handle that? It's an odor orgy from which I've been banished for life.

My olfactory bulb, which receives the signals from those millions of receptors, must be a lazy bum. The few signals that it receives get sent to other parts of the brain where smells are categorized and neurologically linked with our past experiences. But the few signals that I receive get filed straight away.

I don't know why—and I'm tempted to pay a surprise visit to Dr. Axel and Dr. Buck in New York to find out—but the few smells that do manage to filter through my nasal passages remain in my olfactory memory for quite some time. Usually, smells are forgotten shortly after they are experienced. But that's not the case with me.

At times it's rather pleasant. The scent of wet grass after a rainstorm always brings me back to my childhood in Mexico City . . . although this time, the rain is falling in Miami. And it's quite a beautiful thing to keep that scent hanging in my mind all day, and—sometimes—on into the next. My memories of smells flicker back and forth, like a lightbulb about to burn out.

The fetid smell of cigarette smoke becomes a rich elixir when mixed with that of men's aftershave. It's the combination that most reminds me of my father. Somehow, my nose left that little connection intact, left me the gift of my father's smell. He died several years ago, but his scent is etched into my mind. That focus is one of the marvelous advantages of my impaired sense of smell.

The disadvantage is that certain smells persist long after I would have liked to forget them. As I mentioned in the previous letter, I once had to spend days surrounded by the crushing putrefaction of a Kuwaiti morgue. Or that strange sensation of inhaling dust, cement, and human ash after the terrorist attacks on the Twin Towers in New York. Less painful is the smell of the damp carpet that got me through the hardest days of my life as an immigrant in Los Angeles. Can you imagine what it would be like to walk around inundated by these smells for days on end?

When I feel trapped by such things, I rip off my clothes, go someplace new, and incessantly wash my nose. But plain water isn't enough. Nor is alcohol, perfume, or Vicks VapoRub. Constantly smelling death, tragedy, and pain is simply torture.

My battered nose does what it wants to with me, and it takes me to certain places without my permission. Sometimes, at a meeting or at work, for example, my nose will take me some place very far away. And no matter how hard I try to concentrate, the memory of an old smell takes me away with it. I'm a slave to the few odors that are logged in my brain, and I dance to whatever beat they tap out.

〜 **And no matter how hard I try to concentrate, the memory of an old smell takes me away with it. I'm a slave to the few odors that are logged in my brain, and I dance to whatever beat they tap out.**

It is certain that my severely compromised sense of smell has affected my sense of taste as well. Not being able to smell your food takes a good deal of pleasure out of the act of eating. And so, I prefer strongly seasoned dishes to more bland ones. Anything with pepper, mustard, salt, lemon, or chili excites my palate. And the strange thing is that I tend to eat the things that I enjoyed before my first operation. So it should come as no surprise, then, that I'm a true avocado addict.

As when I was a child, my tastes make up a limited, specific list, including tacos *al pastor* (where the meat is sliced off a Middle Eastern–style rotisserie), ceviche, pozole (a type of pre-Colombian stew), shrimp, some greasy fried eggs, and—above all—a slice of buttered bread, which I still love. It's quite possible that those tastes and smells I learned in my mom's kitchen are the only ones that still register in my beat-up olfactory system under the favorites category.

Eating much else not on the list does not set off the pleasure receptors in my brain the way it could. This also goes a long way to explaining why I'm so skinny. I enjoy certain foods and restaurants; there's no doubt about that. Though I can also skip a meal or two without any real bother. My problem is maintaining weight, not losing it. I always lose weight when I'm traveling, especially if it's for work. I end up forgetting that I do, in fact, have to eat. But there are compensations.

My nearly nonexistent sense of smell and my inability to enjoy flavors have heightened my senses of sight, hearing, and touch. Though I played classical guitar for years, I don't have a musical ear, but it is still very sensitive. Anything and everything will wake me up. I sleep with my ears wide open. Every night I hear the sounds of the house settling, despite the fact that it's relatively new. And thanks to the discipline involved in my work—

where I hear the instructions given by the producers through a tiny earpiece—I can follow two and sometimes three conversations at the same time. Believe me, it's good for eavesdropping.

But my eyes and fingers might be even more sensitive than my ears.

Seeing and touching. That's enough for me. They're my most important pleasures. My eyes and hands have taken over the jobs that my nose was never able to perform, and they have become experts in the fine subtleties of locating and recovering hidden objects. I've learned to live by sight out of simple necessity, and not much escapes my range of vision.

Every day I practice "the art of noticing"—which goes well beyond simple observation—and refers to the Polish journalist Ryszard Kapuscinski. The images I keep in my mind have, for me, the same suggestive power that smells hold for other people. And if those images are accompanied by a tactile memory, then I'm complete. It's almost like I'm living the moment all over again.

Those who know me, know that I see so many things because I don't have a full set of tools to work with. When I observe something, when I take note of something, I'm saving it to my internal hard drive.

I'll end this letter—something of a twisted ode to my labyrinthine nose—with two of the best odoriferous memories that luckily I do remember: the way each of you smelled when you were babies. They drive me crazy. There's no scent more extraordinary anywhere else on earth.

Fully aware of my olfactory limitations, I would lean in as close as I could to your hair and your little faces so that I could take in as much as possible your incredible, peaceful aroma. And I managed to do it. Though it wasn't easy—my nose doesn't readily accept new members into its exclusive scent club. It doesn't welcome new scents that arrive after my first surgery. But for you, it made an exception . . . congratulations!

> ⌁ **Fully aware of my olfactory limitations, I would lean in as close as I could to your hair and your little faces so that I could take in as much as possible your incredible, peaceful aroma.**

Despite the tortuous and inexplicable way in which my olfactory mausoleum works, the way you each smelled as babies has entered into my system. I can't always call them up voluntarily, but every so often they emerge without warning.

When that happens, I don't have anything to look at. I close my eyes, stick my hands in my pockets, and breathe in pure tranquility. That particular, unmistakable, and dearly loved smell of you two as babies is, for me, the nature of peace and happiness. And the best part of all is that it never leaves. It's a part of me.

It's at times like that when I'll say to myself, with a smile on my face, what more could I ask for?

Superstrong hugs,
your nonsmelling father

AN E-MAIL TO PAOLA

FROM: DAD

TO: PAO

SUBJECT: HOW NOT TO BE A LONG-DISTANCE DAD

Hey Pao,

So, we've just finished dinner with your friends at that Italian restaurant on Broadway for your birthday. I cannot believe you're already twenty. Remember when you said to me, "Dad, I want to be twenty, and then stay that age forever"? This I completely understood. After all, who wouldn't want to be twenty for the rest of their life?

Sometimes, I have to admit, it's a little hard to grasp the fact that this lovely young woman sitting next to me at dinner is my little girl. I know it's a tired cliché, but it's all gone by *so* fast. And when I give your arm a squeeze or you lay your head on my shoulder, I am overwhelmed by this very innate paternal pride. It's an odd sort of pride, this fatherhood thing. It's not pride at something that's been won, like a soccer game, it is a pride that I've arrived at *with* you, more like a marathon.

⌒ It's an odd sort of pride, this fatherhood thing. It's not pride at something that's been won, like a soccer game, it is a pride that I've arrived at *with* you, more like a marathon.

I'm pretty convinced that half of the time we don't even recognize how much we do support each other, how much our success is buoyed by the other. It's extraordinary how much I've come to rely upon you, as a grown-up individual with your own wisdom to share, your own excellent advice to give. But in so many ways, you're still my little girl.

I'd have to be pretty crazy to try and toss you up on my shoulders like we did when you were a kid, when we'd hug and I'd give you a kiss on the cheek or on your forehead, you were such a cute kid. The real joy in those exchanges was that you could share with me the magical feeling that everything fits into a hug, and that you felt like the most loved and protected girl in the world while I felt like the most complete and protective father of all. Corny sentiments like these remind me of that song that you and I would sing in the car: "You've got the most beautiful green eyes . . ."

Oof, dinner. My stomach's about to burst . . . those potatoes were huge, and that dessert was so incredibly rich, but not so much that we couldn't get it down in three bites. We ordered the same entrée: a steak fit for a caveman, which was really great, huh? Cooked medium, not too juicy, just the way we like it . . . something to give us a little energy so we could face that freezing New York City weather, *brrr*. I know you like living there in the city, and I know I would too if I were twenty and going to an incredible college with really sharp professors and surrounded by all my pals—even if it is so cold! It's your life, not mine, but I enjoy it as if it were my own.

When I was your age, a little younger, I had the opportunity to go to university in England. I knew my parents didn't have the money, so I asked my grandma, who was the only one who had a little nest egg put away. She didn't want to loan it to me, and I was crushed. I thought that if my grandpa was still alive that he would've lent it to me, since money from the ranch that he had and sold (with all those orange groves, walnut trees, and avocado trees) surely provided enough for my education. But it wasn't to be. None of the grandkids saw so much as an avocado pit or a walnut shell. And you know what? It made me resolute. It made me stronger. There are challenges in life that leave a serious mark on you, and that was one of them for me. I promised myself that in the future I would never have to ask anyone for money again, or have to tell someone asking me that I couldn't help them.

That's one of the reasons it makes me so happy to see you so thrilled in New York, because I was able to keep the promise I made always to be able to provide for my family. When I made that promise, you weren't even born yet, you know, and I wasn't even planning to have kids, since I was so focused on other things at the time, but the fact is that once you were born, I wanted you to have everything that I never did. And here we are, in the big city, celebrating your birthday, and I couldn't be happier.

I look at you and I see myself. It's not that I want you to follow in my footsteps . . . not at all. It's awesome when you come to me with questions about politics or current events, or when you e-mail me one of the papers you're writing at school. I see myself in your doubts, in your anxieties, in that inexplicable hesitancy to speak up in class, and especially in that crazy feeling that you've got the world in the palm of your hand. When I was in my twenties and even into my thirties and forties, I looked at the world the same way. I felt like I could take a big bite out of it as if it were one of the steaks we had tonight. I still feel that way sometimes. I want you to know that I see and understand these concerns you have, and that I feel them, too.

I'm thrilled that you're such an accomplished traveler, that you have such an incredible ability to adapt yourself to any situation, that nothing ever really shocks or startles you, that you take things as they come without judging them . . . that's truly a great gift. I can see how your friends (and even some of mine) feel happy just being around you. You project this vibe that your world is very broad, and that it's got room for everyone—with that world vision, you've already won half the battle. Don't ever change that: It's one of your best qualities. I didn't raise you to be a successful woman; I taught you to be a complete human being, and as far as I'm concerned that's even better. I know that you've already had to face your share of sexism, and I know that you'll never let anyone put limits on you for the simple (and marvelous) fact of your being a woman.

Since you are a woman of the world, in no corner of it should you feel like you don't belong. Well, of course, I'm exaggerating a little bit, but you get the idea, right? You have an astonishingly open mind. And you're like many other members of your generation: skeptical without being cynical, much more practical than my generation (which, as you say, is sometimes prehistoric), and you have a sense of solidarity and humor that has been lacking in those of us who came before you.

Sometimes I worry that that ability to adapt yourself to what-ever comes your way was an involuntary part of your upbringing and all the transplantation that ensued. First from Los Angeles to Madrid, then from Miami to Madrid, and now from Madrid to New York—bouncing around has always been a part of your life. You don't know what it means to be still. Moving, shifting, changing is your constant . . . your father here, your mother there, a brother here, a sister there. . . . but I want you to know that I never planned such a life for you, nobody thought it would turn out like it did, but in the end there's just nothing left to do but accept your parents' decisions. Not the easiest thing to do, huh? You were the one most affected by it, and the one least able to make decisions affecting your own future.

Paola, I've never dreaded a day quite as much as when you went to live with your mother in Madrid. I hated it, all of it. I hated the awful circumstances that motivated your trip, I hated that we had come to the point of a forced separation, I hated living without you, I hated being thousands of miles away from you, I hated myself for having generated that situation, I hated the days that would go by without any news of you, I hated having to imagine you at school and then not being able to pick you up in the afternoon the way fathers are supposed to for their daughters, I hated the evenings when I couldn't help you with your homework, take you to the movies, or watch you at basketball practice, I hated the nights when I wasn't able to tuck you in, and the nights when I slept not know-ing that you were sick or studying or watching TV, just counting down the days until we would see each other again. I hated every moment I wasn't spending with you. Even now, it still fills me with anguish and anger and pain to revisit those worst days of my life. Yes, Paola, they were the worst days of my life. When I meet moth-ers or fathers in similar situations, my heart breaks for them.

It was only in the mornings where I found a bit of consolation, foolishly thinking that because of the difference in time zones between the U.S. and Spain, you wouldn't be up for another six, seven, or eight hours, and that meant there were fewer hours in the day to endure. I just couldn't stand the idea of us both being out and about at the same time, and yet not seeing each other.

When you were still just a child, you recognized the wrongness of all of it. "Papá," you asked me, "why don't you come live in Madrid? There's TV work you could do there, too." It was as if you were saying, If you love me as much as you say you do, then why don't you come live with me? I gave you every explanation possible: that my job was based in Miami, that you can't move an entire network to Madrid, that I didn't have documentation allowing me to work in Spain, that my career was starting to take off in the U.S., and that going to Spain would be professional suicide . . . besides, we spoke every weekend, and we always saw each other on vacation. Even at nine years old, you'd accuse me of using empty words.

I gave you completely logical answers, but I never admitted to you what I really felt: that inside I felt broken, and that there was nothing I wanted more in this world than to be able to live with you, to watch you grow, to help you, to be a father who was present day and night. I tried to compensate for the distance with presents and surprises, dozens of packages filled with candy and toys; I went from store to store and carefully selected things I thought you might like. Your grandparents were my mules, ferrying you gifts all year-round. And you brought me so much joy every time you would send me one of your drawings or one of your first handwritten letters.

Sundays were the worst. I'd lie down on the couch in the afternoon, buried in a wave of sadness. I tried to keep my spirits up, playing soccer or working out in the mornings, but eventually those Sunday afternoons would get me down. I'd stare at the TV, read every single page of the newspaper, and sleep without dreaming through nights that seemed interminable until Monday finally came like a blessing. I'd go to work exhausted, with dark circles under my eyes, but at least I'd gotten through another Sunday. For a few more days, at least.

When friends and family saw me, I knew they were thinking: "There goes the saddest father on earth, poor Jorge, with his daughter so far away." I spent those days thinking about what I'd done wrong, about the moment when my life became so painful, about the tragedy of having the one person I love the most so very far away from me. It was torture. And the hardest part of all was at the beginning, which I imagine was so confusing and complicated for a three-year-old, speaking to your father only by telephone, and it was never enough. I'd ask how you were, hiding the heartbreak in my voice so that you wouldn't feel sad. And now, so many years later, it's happening to me again. I'm crying. I'll just never forget.

> ∿ **And the hardest part of all was at the beginning, which I imagine was so confusing and complicated for a three-year-old, speaking to your father only by telephone, and it was never enough.**

Even being so far away, I came to see you whenever I possibly could, showing up in Madrid, staying in a hotel. But we were able to overcome the impersonal nature of the place and make it into our refuge; for a few days, at least, that space belonged to just the two of us, complete with pillow forts and room service sundaes.

When I went to that town near Barcelona to watch you play

in a basketball tournament—that pretty sweet, huh? (see, I still sometimes try to talk like you)—I lost my voice from so much cheering. Since you were a teenager I pictured myself going to the Olympics and watching you compete as an athlete . . . you were so great (well, you still are, really), and I would think to myself, my poor kid, with her dad pushing her to be an Olympian. I thought then, and I still believe now, that there's nothing you can't do if you really want to. There's a reason that I still put up a fight on the basketball court. Yes, I know that you beat me last time, but wait till you're home next and I'll get my revenge! Winner plays your brother, okay?

Can you stick with your dad a little bit longer here? When a father is separated from his daughter for whatever reason, the most important thing is that they maintain total confidence in the other. Do you remember how, ever since you were just a baby, I would always tell you that "promises are meant to be kept"? I did that because I wanted to give you the certainty of knowing that—if I told you I'd see you on this or that date—that I would do it. I don't know how I did it, but I always kept those promises. Sometimes I might have been a day or two late if I got caught up in something at work, a last-minute flight, or an interview; other times I would show up early, but one way or another I got there when I said I would.

Our relationship has often been defined by that effort to stay together. I know your life in Madrid was very fulfilling, with tons of friends and activities and a cultural life that you wouldn't have found in Miami. I'm sure you got a more complete, well-rounded education there. Visiting you, I realized just how wonderfully you were growing up—a strong girl despite (or perhaps because of) the absence of your father.

I remember feeling a hole forming in my stomach every time

we had to say good-bye at the airport, and it would take me several days to get back to feeling somewhat normal. Even after so many years, when we were all accustomed to the distance and the phone calls and the summer vacations and the packages and the marvelous epistolary miracle of e-mail, it still gnawed at me. When you came to the difficult decision (well, it was difficult for you, anyway) to return to Miami for high school and to get ready for college, it was just about the best news I've ever received.

You uprooted yourself from your European life—filled with parties and friends and energy and things to do in the streets—to move to a pedestrian-unfriendly city whose cultural life doesn't even compare with Madrid and where you didn't have very many close friends. It was brave, and I admired you. Me, I was over the moon.

Those two years were over in a heartbeat. And they weren't without their challenges; we certainly had our spats. I wasn't the saintly father whom you'd constructed in your mind, and I had to learn how to live with a teenage daughter who—in a lot of ways—was not the doting little girl I'd been expecting. But it was wonderful always having you right there in the next room. I finally felt balanced having you in the same place as me. If only you had wanted to go to college in Miami.

Finding the right school for you pretty much became my personal mission, and those early rejection letters were a tough blow to deal with. However, as always happens with the challenges you face, it turned out wonderfully. You matriculated at a great school in the great city of New York. Which meant—once again—that we would be apart. I knew it was inevitable, and that time around I approached it from a much different perspective than the one I had many years before when you left for Madrid. I consoled myself that at the very least, we were in the same country—hell, even the same time zone.

Still, that doesn't put us entirely in synch, and our relationship has changed a lot over the years. No longer am I the father of a minor, and no longer do you have to ask permission or consult me about the choices you make. Fortunately, the joy lies in being able to connect about the important stuff *and* the minutiae. The simple fact that we talk to each other about who you or I might be going out with is a small triumph, don't you think? A lot of dads can't say the same thing.

I also know that I've made some big mistakes with you. First of all, it took me way too long to realize that you were becoming a woman and that I should stop treating you so much as a child. I'm sorry it took me so long to digest these things, but I'm doing my homework and I'm making strides all the time, I promise.

I sometimes don't tell you enough about the less pleasant things in my life, rationalizing that you have enough things to worry about. How and when should I have gone about telling you that my marriage wasn't working out? I still don't know, but I do know that I should have said something sooner. Instead, the day I left, you walked into my room to find the closet empty and the computer gone from my desk. It was an awful move on my part, really horrible timing; and instead of shielding you from worry, I caused an abundance of it.

Big mistake. It won't happen again. But the experience taught us each something. We had very complicated talks; in fact, I think that for the first time we had hard, totally honest conversations. For the first time in my life, I was able to talk to you as an adult about these problems, confident in the fact you understood that you and your brother are the most important people in my life.

I'm sure there are a thousand things that I could have done better with you. I'm not going to worry about them now. Looking back on it all, the truth is that we've turned out pretty good, right? There's a photo of the two of us that I've always loved: You were just a few months old—you hadn't even started crawling yet—and I had just finished giving you your bottle. We were at your mother's cousins' house, it was a splendid afternoon on the patio overlooking the canal, and you had fallen asleep on my chest . . . drooling all over my green shirt. Someone, I can't remember who, came up from behind and snapped a picture . . . your face, with your little sleepy eyes, was resting up against my shoulder, and I looked happy and at peace and complete. It must have been one of the first pictures ever taken of the two of us together. And you know what? Twenty years later, at that restaurant, with you by my side, I felt much the same way.

Happy birthday. This morning I sang you the *mañanitas* song that King David sang for his beautiful girls. I knew that you would be laughing when you heard my glorious singing voice belting out that traditional Mexican birthday song . . . you laughed, and I loved it. I can still make you laugh. You still move me. And that is more than enough to fill my heart.

∼ **I knew that you would be laughing when you heard my glorious singing voice belting out that traditional Mexican birthday song . . . you laughed, and I loved it. I can still make you laugh. You still move me. And that is more than enough to fill my heart.**

Always with you, whether near or far,
your dad

PS . . . when you get a chance, give me a call, or at least a text message, to let me know you're okay . . . okay?

TO NICOLÁS, MY BEST BUDDY

My Nico:

You're sleeping, so I'm taking advantage of the chance to write to you.

We're exhausted. It was a standard Saturday: You woke up at sunrise, before seven in the morning (I can hear you in the other room playing on the computer before moving to the TV, surely thinking to yourself, "When is that lazy dad of mine ever going to get up?"). Eventually, you just can't wait anymore, and you jump into my bed. What a shock! Yes, good morning to you, Nicolás.

We're not much for sit-down breakfasts, but that day was different. You had a chocolate chip muffin and a few strips of bacon. It's the Nico-combo. I have no idea how you can eat that in the morning, but somehow it's your favorite.

No sooner had you finished your breakfast than did you jump out of your chair and head to your bedroom to get dressed. Your soccer game wouldn't kick off for another two hours, but you wanted to be ready and waiting in uniform and those new cleats, a pair of red Adidas boots that you assiduously clean, polish, and admire as if they were the most valuable things in the world. It was the one Christmas present that you wanted most of all.

El fútbol (or soccer, as you call it now) has done some great things for you. It's given you a sense of confidence and assurance that's rare in someone your age. There's definitely a touch of my family's classic timidity in your blood, but you've grown past it, especially on the field.

⌁ **There's definitely a touch of my family's classic timidity in your blood, but you've grown past it, especially on the field.**

The other day you asked me about the first time you ever kicked around a soccer ball, and unless my memory deceives me, it was right after you started walking. At eighteen months you were knocking beach balls around, and shortly thereafter you started coming with me to my Saturday morning soccer games. You and I would play around for awhile, and then you'd sit down and watch the game on the field. Who knew that those games would be such an influence on you?

You weren't quite four yet when you started playing soccer in the street. We bought a set of mini-goals—those white plastic ones, which we still have in the yard—and you were never shy about winning. There's nothing better for building some self-esteem than beating your dad, right? Well, I *may* have let you win those early games, but times are changing: I'm playing hard now, and you're still beating me.

Honestly, this morning you played like a champ. You scored on me three or four times, and I was so proud when your team's coach invited you to play in a later game that same day with much older kids. I was surprised, then, that you said no, but I figured it out soon: You wanted to go home for a quick power snack before lacing up your basketball shoes—and it was onto the day's next athletic endeavor.

As I watched you play, I couldn't help but think about how lucky you were. How lucky we were, actually. You were playing on an indoor, hardwood court, with NBA-quality jerseys, and a referee. And earlier that same morning, you were scoring goals on a lush, green soccer field. How many kids (or adults) in other countries around the world would give anything to see a field like that? It's no surprise that the best basketball players on earth come from here, or that the U.S. men's national soccer team has become one of the ten best squads on the globe.

You lost that game by one basket, and there was no hiding the frustration in your eyes, though you said nothing.

Nico, you're incredibly competitive, and you certainly enjoy winning. I applaud your good sportsmanship. You're an excellent athlete and, despite your size and strength, you never complain when things don't go your way—but I still sense you can't stand losing. And I'm not too sure what to do about that. It's great to see you put out such an effort on the court or on the field—that's what sports are about, right? To test your limits and abilities without any serious consequences, but I know how hard it's going to be for you if you don't learn that winning isn't the most important thing. Well, I'm probably getting ahead of myself. You're only eight years old, and you've got a long way to go yet.

⌐ **It's great to see you put out such an effort on the court or on the field—that's what sports are about, right? To test your limits and abilities without any serious consequences,**

but I know how hard it's going to be for you if you don't learn that winning isn't the most important thing.

I already said this in an e-mail to your sister, but I'll say it here to you as well: I see a lot of myself in you—making me surprised, nervous, and proud all at the same time.

When I watch you playing soccer or basketball, your ease, grace, and skill all move me. I was like that once. Well, perhaps not as strong or as athletic, but I was fast. Plus, we share the same obsession with athletic shoes. We both get a huge kick out of them. And I can't think of a better combination: an athletic son whose dad loves sports. Magic.

The best was that trip to Germany to see the World Cup. You got a jersey for each of the three games we saw—Brazil, Spain, and Paraguay—and in support of the Iberian and Latin American teams. I laughed out loud when we got on the subway and bumped into a group of rowdy, beer-swilling Swedish fans. The Sweden-Paraguay game was that afternoon, and you were wearing your red and white–striped Paraguayan jersey, so you ducked behind me so that the fanatic Swedes wouldn't see you. It was quite amusing. You raised your eyebrows, scrunched up your forehead, and crossed your arms . . . just like I do during moments of tension.

It surprises me just how many of my mannerisms you've inherited, genetically or just by virtue of the amount of time we spend together. Mirroring my tics is automatic for you. For example, did you ever notice that when you're sitting down, you interlace your fingers just the way I do? You eat tacos the same way I do, and you like salsa picante much more than your sister does. We both love tortilla soup, and we both miss our vacations in Acapulco.

On the other hand, I'm already well aware of how you're forging your own path. I've started to see signs of a healthy rebelliousness in you, which—I'm sure—will be turning my gray hair green by the time you're thirteen or fourteen. But that's fine. I'm not concerned. Sometimes I find myself taken aback by the elegance of your speech, the eloquence with which you frame an argument—and you're just a kid! And that is something that I like to see . . . even if it doesn't look like I do at the time. And when I end up frustrated and tired and on the verge of saying "You'll do it because I said so," I try to take a few deep breaths to calm down and see if maybe, just *perhaps*, you're right.

∿ **Sometimes I find myself taken aback by the elegance of your speech, the eloquence with which you frame an argument—and you're just a kid!**

I'm trying to steer the family dynamic away from the unhappy one that I learned from my own parents. We weren't allowed to discuss things in the home. We never learned how to have a dialogue, or how to work disagreements into a conversation. The silence was overwhelming, and the message was clear: It was better to keep quiet than to fight. The problem with that method of resolving conflict is that a lot of unspoken, unsettled issues are building up inside of you. Of course, in a house with five children, it might have been the only system of guaranteeing peace.

When it's just you and me, things are different, aren't they? When one of us gets mad, and even blows up in the end, we wait a little while until we're calm enough to discuss the issue (for as long as necessary) that we're facing. I don't want to leave things hanging so long that they can start to foster resentment, and I prefer to err on the side of too much communication, not too little. Believe me, that's a big change for me. And—just like my dad did with me—I take advantage of time in the car for talking.

When the basketball game was over, you went with me to the barbershop. "Why are you going to cut it," you asked, "when it's already so short?" Well, son, it's a matter of preference. As much as I'd like to grow my hair out like you (only my hair is much, much grayer), I think I prefer not looking like an aging hippie stuck in the wrong decade.

You wear your hair almost the same exact way that I wore mine when I was your age. And you have the same way of flicking it out of your eyes that I had when my hair was long, too. I love the way it looks, and I was the biggest proponent of the idea of growing your hair out as long as possible . . . until the school decided that it was time to get it cut.

In the car, we went back and forth speaking English and Spanish. Or, to be more specific, I spoke to you in Spanish, and you answered me in English. There's no doubt about it: You feel more comfortable in English, and that's perfectly fine. I have a story about your English that might amuse you.

Ever since you were born, we spoke Spanish to you in the home. It was our first language, and yours as well. And you, of course, picked it up quite well. So well, in fact, that I decided to write down some of the more charming ways you've chosen to express yourself in the English language:

As part of a long trip to Italy, we went to see the leaning tower of Pisa. But you had no interest whatsoever in seeing this historic attraction in the middle of summer. You looked at the tower and asked me:

"Dad, is that tower going to fall down?"

"No, Nico," I said. "It's not going to fall down."

"Are we going to see a show there?"

"No, Nico, we're not going to see any shows."

"So what are we looking at then?"

Another time, I was watching an old black-and-white movie when you walked through the room and informed me, "Dad, you should watch something that's been colored in."

⌒ **Another time, I was watching an old black-and-white movie when you walked through the room and informed me, "Dad, you should watch something that's been colored in."**

When we were nagging you about something, you would cover your ears with your hands and say desperately: "Okay, okay, enough already, my head is filling up with words."

You always resisted the idea of sleep. For you, it was a largely worthless endeavor. Ever since you were a newborn, you needed a pacifier to calm you down enough to rest. In fact, that's the basis for one of my most priceless memories. Suddenly, one day, the pacifier went missing. You wandered all over the house, looking for your so-called "minga minga." But we couldn't find it anywhere. "I want my minga minga," you told us all until—finally—we found it. And we also found out that you were saying "minga minga" because that was the sound that the pacifier made when you sucked on it. "Minga minga" it was. Suffice it to say that, for a long time thereafter, the whole world knew you as "minga minga."

But with or without your "minga minga," getting you to sleep was a lot of work. We made up a story almost every night based on a fictitious character named Cocoloco. His legs were so long that he could pick fruit from the trees, play with the birds in the sky, get burned by the sun, and every night he swiped the moon so he could take it to bed with him.

Cocoloco would fall sleep, and sometimes I would, too, out of pure exhaustion. You, on the other hand, wouldn't.

"Sleep here with me," you said, "otherwise I can't dream," warning me of the consequences. "Or I'll sleep with my eyes open." But eventually they would close. For a little while anyway.

You were always an early riser. You would be up at the crack of dawn, and sometimes even earlier. "I'm tired of sleeping," you usually said. "And I can't go back to sleep because I already ran out of dreams."

From time to time, you gave us true lessons in wisdom and common sense. During a particularly long after-dinner discussion that we were having about the possibility of an upcoming trip, you asked, "Why are you always talking about things that you never do?"

"Kids don't do what they don't want to do," you preached. And when we wanted to get you to do something that you didn't want to, you learned a marvelous little phrase, loaded with ambiguity: "I'll go soon, after a little while." After a little while infrequently came.

There were others.

"When does Emilio get here?" I once asked you, about one of your friends.

"When he walks through the door."

You played at "spider killing," which involved drowning spiders with a "water cannon" (your own spit). You asked for impossible things—"Tomorrow will you take me to Australia? Do they have beds there?"; you made zoological observations—"Why do airplanes look like they have rat faces?"; and you had (shall we say) rather mature perceptions—"When I'm as old as Grandpa, will I have hair in my ears?"

You've always been good at coming up with questions that are very difficult to answer, like "Why don't things fall off the planet?" or "How do angels fly?" or "Can I go flying too?"

Everything was going along fine until one day you came up with "caca de bird." Bird poop had marked the end of one linguistic world (Spanish) and the start of a new one (English). But it was to be expected. Most of your friends only spoke English, and the influence from TV was unavoidable.

Your first few weeks of kindergarten were complicated. You spoke very well in Spanish, but your English wasn't quite as good. And that isolated you somewhat from your classmates and made it much more difficult to understand the teacher. Then, one weekend, something clicked, and suddenly you knew that English was the key to getting ahead, to making friends, and to participating in the classroom, and you stopped communicating in Spanish.

It really was impressive. One Friday you were speaking Spanish, and then, somehow, by Monday you had decided on English. Ever since that fateful weekend, you've been living in a bilingual world. I'm wondering here whether you'll read these letters as I wrote them in Spanish, or in their English translation. It's all the same, really, as long as you read them.

~ **It really was impressive. One Friday you were speaking Spanish, and then, somehow, by Monday you had decided**

on English. Ever since that fateful weekend, you've been living in a bilingual world.

Why speak in only one language if you can use two? Multiple languages open borders and, of course, they'll offer you more and more opportunities in a country that is getting ever more diverse and multicultural. Besides, why give up Spanish, the link to your family and your culture?

After the barbershop, we went to the movies. "I feel like seeing a movie, Dad," you said. We ended up seeing an animated film, but you had wanted to see *The Pursuit of Happyness* with Will Smith and his son. The story—in which a father and his son struggle to escape poverty—touched you, and you asked me questions for over two hours. I think that, for the first time, you began to understand how fortunate we've been.

It hasn't always been easy. Ever since I left home, life for you has changed radically. Having to jump from one place to another, dividing up your clothes, your toys, and your emotions, and—toughest and most upsetting of all—seeing your parents permanently separated. How did we ever make it this far? For now, it's enough just to know that we love each other like crazy, that you're not to blame for anything, and that I promise I'll always be there in your life. No matter what.

You're my best buddy.

Just look at how we spent that Saturday. And you know what? It sounds strange to say it, but we spend much more time together now than when I lived at home. I know, it's neither an excuse nor any consolation, but I'm glad to know that we've been able to make something positive out of all this.

When we're together, I'm reminded of the film *Kramer vs. Kramer*. I saw it many, many years ago, well before you were born. It's the story of how a son and his father deal with the events of daily life after a divorce. Some day you'll watch it and laugh. The protagonist, played by Dustin Hoffman, is a disaster in the kitchen; he can't even manage a couple of hotcakes. But during the course of the film, both characters—father and son—become expert cooks. Through that, they come to learn a few things about life. I'm not saying we should both become chefs (though you'd have to admit I'm pretty good with frozen waffles and microwave French fries, right?), but I have actually noticed that we've gotten used to that strange yet affectionate routine of a father and son sharing a house just between the two of them.

I enjoy every moment with you. Believe it or not, I'm still learning how to be a father. I could never aspire to be anything more. And a good part of it is thanks to your sister. Not everything I tried with her ended up working! But I learned: both from our triumphs and our mistakes. And I hope I've done all my homework and learned enough not to repeat the bad stuff. You'll have to be the judge of that.

After the movie, we went to one of your favorite restaurants. Italian, of course. Lately you've been Googling the best Italian restaurants in Miami, though I'm not sure why because you always end up choosing the same ones. And at every one of those restaurants, you always order the same thing: margherita pizza (just sauce and cheese, please, nothing else) or penne pasta alla Bolognese (with extra Parmesan please, a little more, a little more, a little more please, thanks).

Bellies full, hearts content, and many tired bones to drag

around. The day was getting long, and we still had things to do. The moon was up in the Miami sky, and I was looking forward to a few moments of peace. Finally we arrived back home, but you still wanted to go out in the backyard and take some shots on goal. Of course, I couldn't resist. That little space behind the garage where you and I play soccer is indeed hallowed ground. It's where we can connect with each other without saying a word. I'd always wanted a house with a soccer goal in the back . . . though sometimes, in our case, I think that it's actually a soccer goal with a house attached to it.

When it finally got too dark to play, we went inside and looked at some photos that your uncle had e-mailed to us. I showed you my favorite: We were standing together after a 10K road race where you jumped in with me for the home stretch. You were so happy that you jumped over the barrier separating the spectators from the runners and finished the race with me.

And then we came to the cover design for the Spanish edition of this very book, which I proudly showed you. There we were, with you on my right side and Paola on my left.

"Papi, you put me on the cover!" you said, stunned. "That's cool." And you gave me a hug.

Then you left me there, smiling at the computer monitor, and went off to watch some TV. Again, from the other room, I could hear you laughing. You'd recorded one of your favorite shows and were watching it for the umpteenth time. Then, bit by bit, your hearty laughter began to grow more quiet. You were getting tired.

Feet dragging, you followed me up to your room. And despite feeling exhausted, you stuck to your routine, getting into your pj's and brushing your teeth. You have an impressive sense of discipline. Then I turned out the lights, save for the one on your nightstand.

You lay down, I gave you a long hug, and you reached out with your hand so I could squeeze it. And I asked myself how much longer this ritual would last. I realize that when I take you to school in the mornings, you don't like to say good-bye with a hug or a kiss; you prefer to just touch my hand. And the more you grow, the more I expect there will be a greater physical distance between us. That's normal; it's just a sign of independence. But I'm going to miss those childhood hugs. That night, however, everything was as it should be.

We started chatting. It's one of the most opportune moments for such things.

Tired and lying down in bed, we can say things that we might keep more closely guarded during the day.

"What a great day we had today."

"Yeah, Dad, it's been a good day. Stay awhile."

It's been two months now that you've been sleeping alone in your own room. When we first moved into this new house, I would usually sleep on the extra bed in here to keep you company. You were still just a little bit hesitant about sleeping alone in a new home. Plus, my own bedroom was on the ground floor at the other end of the house.

We know that you're growing up, and that means that we each sleep in our own bedrooms. But you know what? I've got something to tell you: The one who struggles the most from not sharing a room together isn't you . . . it's me.

When you sleep, you radiate a sense of peace and tenderness all its own. But it's not going to last much longer. You're on the verge of becoming a man. But in the meantime, your sounds and smells help me to sleep, softly and deeply.

With you always,
your buddy

FEAR OF FLYING

He who is not everyday conquering some fear has
not learned the secret of life.

—RALPH WALDO EMERSON

My children:

You two are on the ground, while I'm at 37,000 feet of altitude. I'm writing this letter while on a long, five-hour flight from Miami to Los Angeles.

I brought my laptop and a stack of notes about some of my worst experiences pertaining to air travel. It's not that I want to emphasize the negatives; rather, I want you both to know how vulnerable I feel when flying.

Flying makes me nervous. My palms sweat. I tense up at the slightest bit of turbulence. This particular flight's takeoff, for example, had its moments. Pilots usually keep the plane's airspeed low for a few seconds after takeoff to keep the noise pollution as low as possible in the areas they fly over. But sometimes that reduction in speed isn't very subtle, and I get alarmed . . . even more so if we happen to be surrounded by clouds heavy with tropical rains.

If the plane moves around much, I'll tighten my seat belt to the point where it's almost hard to breathe. I have the bad (and useless) habit of gripping the armrests with all my strength, as if that will keep anything from happening to me. Sometimes, I wonder if I'm about to rip them off.

And the craziest thing of all is that if I can see even a speck of land from the plane, then somehow I feel just a little bit safer. That's why I always try to get a window seat. As I'm writing this now, I've got some great views of the Florida Keys. They're way off in the distance, with no runways where a Boeing 757 could make an emergency landing, but to me, all terra firma is good terra firma.

Whenever possible, I try to avoid flying at night. There's nothing more disconcerting than to look out a window and see nothing but darkness. Or, even worse, clouds dimly lit by the lights on the plane's wings. And if there's any lightning flashing across the sky in the distance, then that—for me—is the perfect storm. It sounds completely irrational, I know, but I just don't like flying at night or in bad weather.

There aren't very many times when I've been able to enjoy a peaceful flight. I've tried everything. A beer. Or two. Not sleeping the night before. Getting to the airport at the very last minute. Or showing up three hours before boarding, to give me time to prepare myself psychologically. Nothing has ever worked.

There aren't very many times when I've been able to enjoy a peaceful flight. I've tried everything. A beer. Or two. Not sleeping the night before. Getting to the airport at the very last minute. Or showing up three hours before boarding, to give me time to prepare myself psychologically. Nothing has ever worked.

I think there are two things at the heart of my fear of flying. First, I love life, and I'm not ready to say good-bye to it quite yet. And second, I tend to get tremendously stressed out whenever I think about what happens after death. If there is a heaven, I'd like to see the two of you there. And a lot of other people, too. But heaven—if it exists—must be pretty overpopulated.

Clearly, I'm more terrestrial than celestial. Air is not my element. And it may well be because I've had two big scares. I think I've already mentioned them during some after-dinner conversation, though I'm sure I left out a few of the details. So if you'll indulge me here, I'll tell the stories again.

The first of these scares took place in 1991 during the Persian Gulf War. I was on board a military C-130 flight to the city of Dhahran, in Saudi Arabia's eastern province. The thing I remember most about that flight is a violent movement of the plane followed by a rapid descent and turbulence. I couldn't see anything through the tiny side windows, as they were located high up on the fuselage and not accessible by the hundred or so passengers.

Our fear was so great that the producer who was traveling with me came over and took what she called "the last photo of your life." I still have it. I stuck it in my photo album, and now it makes me laugh. I guess it's from the nervousness that the memories bring back. There I am, with very few gray hairs, looking away and gripping my safety belt as if my life depended on it. (Of course, what good would a safety belt do if the plane were about to crash . . . ?)

I look very odd in the photo, as if looking inside myself. It's paralyzing to think that you're living the final moments of your life. I wasn't worried about feeling any pain at the moment of death; rather, I was worried about what came next. I lost control of my body's movements. Some parts—arms, legs, jaw, and stomach—started trembling, while others—my eyes and my mouth—went cold. You want to cry with fear and shout with desperation all at the same time. Deep down, there's that tiny flicker of hope that you just might make it out of there alive, and you don't want to mess that up. How ridiculous it is to worry about maintaining your composure right down to the bitter end!

The plane was shuddering violently, like a giant blender. Some of the passengers were shouting, and an Egyptian pilot who was sitting near me got up and ran through the cabin in clear desperation. These were not good signs.

I didn't know what was going to happen, so I started writing you a letter, Paola.

I wrote that I was in a military aircraft heading into a war zone—Saddam Hussein's Iraqi military had just invaded Kuwait, and the United States was about to respond in kind and liberate that little country—and that you wouldn't have the slightest idea of what ended up happening to your father. I was carrying a few pictures of you, and suddenly I became enormously saddened when I thought about the possibility of never seeing you again. You had just turned four years old. I wrote that I could see a ray of light shining down through one of the little windows high up in the cabin, and I imagined that, somehow, it was you.

It wasn't all that long ago when you called me on the phone after finding that letter in one of my books. I knew that some day you'd read it. But as I was writing it, I never even imagined that, many years later, we'd be talking it about over the phone. Yes, it's all very melodramatic, and with the perspective of time, it even seems a bit exaggerated, but that frightful scare on the plane made me lose my center of being. And the only consolation I had in that moment of panic was you.

To make a long story short, the plane was able to land despite the failure of one of its left wing engines. They repaired it right there on the airstrip and—much to my dismay—we prepared to take off again in just a few minutes.

What was I going to do? I couldn't exactly call my producer and refuse to reboard the plane. I had already complained in the beginning, but the station had invested many thousands of dollars in me covering the Gulf War. Thinking back on it, I should have walked away. But at that time, it was still early in my career, and I had great aspirations of being a successful journalist. So I bit my tongue, took a deep breath, and got back on the darn thing. Hindsight being what it is, it all seems absurd now. At the time, though, I barely even questioned it. I'd have to be crazy to have changed my plans.

I don't like flying because I feel like I have no control. I've read all the statistics about how air travel is safer than driving. But I'll still argue that if the engine fails in a car, you can just pull over and call a tow truck. But if the engine fails in a plane . . .

The fact is that much of my life is dependent upon airplanes. I have to go where the news is. Period. And after logging over a million miles in the air, I've memorized every sound and movement that a plane can make. That's put me just a little bit more at ease. It doesn't matter anymore where I'm seated, as I've convinced myself that I'll be able to see outside no matter where I am.

I know that sometimes, as a father, I might seem invincible to you. Or that you might never even think that something bad could ever happen to me. You must be saying to yourselves, "He's already done it all so many times that he must know it all by now." I feel I should let you know that it's not really like that.

It's great that you think of me as being indestructible, if it gives your lives a certain sense of security and continuity. And at one point in my life, I thought that my own parents were capable of doing anything. Maybe we have such thoughts because, as children, it's impossible to think about a life without your parents. But the fact is—and it pains me to say so—that your father is made of flesh and bone, and sometimes he's simply scared to death.

The second time when I thought my life might end was on board a tiny little aircraft operated by the Venezuelan air force.

Venezuelan president Hugo Chávez had promised me an interview. But it wasn't in Caracas, where we were staying, but rather in the small town of Guarumito, in the state of Táchira, near the border with Colombia. Out in the boondocks.

Chávez wanted to be seen as a man of the people. It was February of 2000, and he hadn't yet let all his power go to his head. (Years later, he would become impossible to interview, refusing to listen to anybody except himself. But that's another story, and one not worth retelling now.)

It wasn't yet nine in the morning, and the small prop plane, piloted by two young Venezuelan soldiers, was flying at some 15,000 feet of altitude. Soon, we noticed that a burning smell and white smoke were beginning to fill the cabin. Despite the shouts of protest from seven of the eight passengers on board—one civil servant was still asleep—the pilots refused to make an emergency landing and continued their climb up to 24,000 feet.

The pilot informed us that "we have our orders" and those were to take us to the La Fría airport, where President Chávez was waiting. But the cabin continued to fill with a hot, off-white smoke. The pilot was as stubborn as an ox. How could his "orders" preclude an emergency landing? I worried that he was insane. It seemed obvious to his passengers that the plane was on fire and had to land immediately. But the stoic pilot and co-pilot flatly refused to budge. You can imagine the frustration we all felt. We were going to die because of the imprudence of two inexperienced soldiers. On that particular occasion, my natural suspicions of all things military were confirmed.

Finally—choking on smoke and terrified at the possibility of the small plane going down in flames—we were able to convince the two stubborn pilots to make an emergency landing. They grudgingly agreed, though still unconvinced. With a very macho attitude, they made us feel as though we were true cowards, unable to take even a mild dose of rigor. But our fears turned out to be justified.

The plane touched down at the military base in Barquisimeto. And that's where we come to the point of this story.

While my stomach was twisting itself into knots and my extremities were trembling out of control, I was thinking about the two of you. It seemed so absurd to risk ever seeing you two again in the pursuit of a quasi-dictator located in some place that doesn't even appear on some maps. And it didn't escape my attention that the two pilots might be more afraid of Chávez's anger at not delivering us to the governmentally prescribed area on time than of dying in a fiery plane crash. In their stubbornness, they could easily have ended the lives of myself and my companions. And, by extension, they could have destroyed your lives as well. Such madness.

~ **And it didn't escape my attention that the two pilots might be more afraid of Chávez's anger at not delivering us to the governmentally prescribed area on time than of dying in a fiery plane crash.**

95

I've always had this dilemma:

On the one hand, there's nothing I want more than to spend time with the two of you, but on the other hand, I love my job, and it requires me to travel to strange, far-off places. It's also what enables us to live.

At the heart of these two anecdotes is a lesson about fear. It's important to recognize it. Naturally, it's your first sign of danger. Fear prepares us for situations that might push us to our limits. These two situations have enabled me to get to know myself better. Of course, nobody wants to feel vulnerable and weak. But there comes a time when—thanks to your intensity in the face of fear—you can make it out on top.

There are certain fears in the face of which you can really do nothing but prepare for the inevitable. That's how I felt on those two airplanes. However, there are other fears that, once you identify them, you can face. That goes for public speaking or interviewing for a job, making a new friend, or just simply doing something you've never done before.

The trick is understanding your fears, wherever they may come from, and changing your behavior when possible.

In the end, I've tried to cut down on the number of trips I take so I can spend more time at home. And I think that, to a good degree, I've managed to do that. Nevertheless, I can't be a journalist and be shut up at home at the same time. It's just not possible. I live in the midst of this unavoidable internal conflict of being a journalist and a father at the same time.

I'm not telling you these aerial stories to scare you or even to bore you; rather, I just want you both to know that—even during the most tense moments of my life—my first thoughts are of you. My children.

When life moves into the realm of the almost, I seek refuge

with my children. And I want them to know that. In that, I'm like any other dad.

It's not easy to meld those two jobs: journalism and fatherhood. You can't imagine how complicated it is to care for a family and always to be there for them, while on the other hand the world of news is clamoring for your attention as well.

I'll give you an example. When a group of terrorists hijacked planes and crashed them in New York, Washington, and Pennsylvania on September 11, 2001, my first impulse was to run to your school, Nicolás, and call Paola (who, at the time, was studying in Madrid). But I couldn't. Everything was in an emergency state. I first learned about the multiple attacks, which had caused the deaths of nearly three thousand people, after a pleasant, forty-minute jog down a beautiful, tree-lined promenade.

The office was urgently trying to reach me, I was being bombarded with phone calls from radio stations all over Latin America, and I only had a couple of minutes to shower and pack a suitcase. I knew that my life—and that of millions of people—had been turned upside down, and it would probably never be the same. And my first thought was to be with you, to give you both a big hug and assure you that I would be there to protect you. I wanted to say to you that your own personal world would not change—that the whole planet itself could collapse—but I would always be there for you and that you could count on me always.

The reality of the situation was something else. I could not be with you two. I simply couldn't. I had no choice but to run to the station where—I knew—I'd be spending the next few weeks in uninterrupted coverage. I also knew that I'd have to go to New York, and that I'd have no idea when I'd be able to return. The only thing I wanted was to be with you, to hug you both until we could all fall asleep. But I simply couldn't.

To make matters worse, I couldn't even say good-bye. Something breaks inside of you when your heart begs to be with your children and yet, for some reason, you cannot. It must not be easy to have a father like me. I haven't always been where I should have. But many, many times, I simply don't know how to divide myself up into pieces.

Just for a moment, I forget that I'm flying.

Soon I reach the mountains surrounding Los Angeles, soaring across the magnificent Pacific Ocean and the beaches where people go out to sunbathe every single day. How could anyone not feel at peace with this view?

There are only a few minutes before we begin our descent, but only now do I realize that I've been flying while writing about my fear of flying. And instead of focusing my attention on the slightest sound or inkling of imminent death on the plane, I've been describing this picture of the two of you. And what's more . . . my palms aren't even sweaty. Maybe I've been a bit unfair about the whole flying thing. It's taken me to places far beyond those I even imagined, and—above all—it's brought me home as well. Every time.

So maybe—and quite unexpectedly—I've found a way to fly in peace.

> *I love you on the ground, at 37,000 feet*
> *of altitude, and everywhere in between,*
>
> *Paps*

PS . . . we landed!

MY HOME AWAY FROM HOME

~

Home is where one starts from.

—T. S. ELIOT

For my kids, who won't be kids for much longer:

I am from two countries.

And I can be. I don't have to choose.

I've spent twenty-five years in the United States, and twenty-five years in Mexico City.

Once, during an interview, I asked the Chilean novelist Isabel Allende if she felt more at home in Chile (where she grew up) or in the United States (where she's lived now for many years). And her answer was loaded with wisdom and common sense. I don't have to choose, she said, I am from two countries.

I feel the same way.

I fit perfectly into a multiethnic, multicultural, multiracial, and multilingual society. We come here from all walks of life.

The United States is a unique place where foreigners cease to be foreign.

You must understand this perfectly, Paoli. You are both American and Spanish.

Feeling compelled to choose a country is irrational, forced, and absurd. Plus, it's totally unnecessary. You are the best example of a globalized citizen in a globalized world. You are a woman of our times.

It's getting harder and harder to find pure identities. We're becoming more mixed. We're all mestizos. Your heart pumps Mexican blood along with Cuban, Spanish, Native American, Puerto Rican, American, and—if you dig deep enough—you'll find a bit of Italian and Irish as well.

Here in the twenty-first century, there's no more inexact science than trying to classify people ethnically.

I am profoundly Mexican—it's both impossible and unthinkable to tear out those roots—but at the same time I've learned to love, respect, and be grateful to the United States. But here in the U.S., many people view me simply as "Hispanic" or "Latino." Just yesterday, in fact, someone thought I was from Bogotá, Colombia, because of my manner of speaking. Other times, I've been thought to be Ecuadoran, Bolivian, and even a light-skinned Salvadoran.

My Spanish accent, almost neutral now after the years of reporting I've done, complicates things further. Sometimes when I travel to Mexico, many people don't even believe that I actually am Mexican, or they believe I've become "gringified," which is a form of rejection. It makes me feel, in the words of Kundera, like the "great traitor." The message is clear: You don't belong here.

In other words, sometimes I don't belong anywhere, while other times I'm from two separate places.

⌁ In other words, sometimes I don't belong anywhere, while other times I'm from two separate places.

I am, indeed, an immigrant, and I'll die still feeling like one.

Anyone who leaves home always feels a certain resistance to being categorized. Labels don't stick to us very well, because we defy almost all of them. The only one that we will always carry is the one that reads—that shouts, really—that we left our home country. Many times in leaving, we've effectively torn up our return tickets. Sometimes, when we want to return, we can have trouble reading the place from where we came. It's as if, without realizing it, we've become someone else.

Professor Edward Said, who lived in Palestine, Lebanon, and Egypt before immigrating to New York, said that "I occasionally experience myself as a cluster of flowing currents." He preferred that to "the idea of having a single solid identity." As he wrote in his autobiography, "With so many dissonances in life, I have learned to prefer being not quite right and out of place."

I'm quoting him here because I feel the same way. After so many changes, so many travels, and so much juggling of two languages, I've lost that single Mexican identity. I'm more, and I'm less. At the same time. I am, as Said says, many currents coming together.

You have heard me say this before, but the United States has given me opportunities that Mexico could not. Paola and Nicolás (written like that, without the "h" of a Nicholas and with an accent over the "a"), you were born here in the U.S., and I know that you both are proud of your country. That's how it should be. It's a sad thing when someone is embarrassed by the country they belong to. It speaks poorly of the person, and poorly of the country.

I came to the United States because I did not want to be a victim. I didn't want to be a slave to circumstance. I couldn't wait any longer. For what? For the death of a president? For a complete change in the system of government? For a complete and total freedom of the press? No, I just couldn't wait for all that. Mexico was about to be built up, and it was strangling me.

So I left. It was right before my twenty-fifth birthday. The catalyst was a case of censorship at the TV station where I worked. But it wasn't just me whom they had censored. They censored us all. In my case, the boss disapproved of a series of interviews I did with two critics of Mexico's presidential system, and he asked me to cut them from the report. I declined to do that, and I also refused to revise my script. So, of course, they sacked me. Or, to be technical about it, I resigned before they could fire me. I allowed myself that bit of pleasure. Not too long ago, while organizing the garage, I found my letter of resignation. A point of pride, it made me feel good to read it again.

So, I had my pride, which was great, and no job, which was less so. And you know the rest of the story: I sold my old red VW, withdrew my meager savings from the bank, got myself a student visa, and went to Los Angeles. I took only what I could carry with my own two hands.

I completely changed my life in a matter of weeks. I didn't exactly know what I wanted, but I definitely knew what I didn't want: to live in a country where you can't say things openly, to be a poor, censored journalist, to be forced to take orders from arrogant, pedantic bosses in Mexico, and—above all—I didn't want to wait for things to change.

I was in a hurry.

The first year was the toughest. I took classes in television and journalism at UCLA while I looked for work. Despite a few Mexican friends I met in L.A., I felt very alone. I could no longer stand to listen to the Mexican music I used to enjoy so much, and I found myself flipping from station to station or just turning off the radio completely. The music depressed me; it reminded me of how far away I was.

I quickly learned that the first thing an immigrant sacrifices when he goes to another country is his sense of camaraderie. The sense of solitude and loneliness is crushing. I must have asked myself a thousand times, "What am I doing here?" You find yourself wondering whether leaving your home country was the right thing to do. Nothing moves you. You feel like you're trapped in a hole. But eventually you remember why you left in the first place, and you begin to make some headway.

> ∿ I quickly learned that the first thing an immigrant sacrifices when he goes to another country is his sense of camaraderie. The sense of solitude and loneliness is crushing.

Exactly one year into my stay, and thanks to a work permit that I obtained after finishing my studies, I got a job in a local Los Angeles TV station. Channel 34 was a small operation; the only one broadcasting in Spanish at the time. Today, it's one of the most widely viewed stations in the city. Who would ever have thought that twenty-some years later, I would still be working at the same company?

Besides the stability the job provided, it also enabled me to circle the globe several times over in the pursuit of news and the people who make that news. If I had stayed in Mexico, our story—both yours and mine—would be a very different one.

How could I not be grateful to this country?

I learned English very fast. I had some of the basics down, thanks to my required classes back in elementary school, but for all intents and purposes, I was starting from scratch. But I had no doubts about it: If I wanted to be successful in the U.S., I'd have to learn the language that the majority of the people speak. And I did. With an accent and with the occasional grammatical slipup, perhaps, but I learned it.

The first thing that caught my attention about this country was its diversity. Here, everyone originated from somewhere else. The United States is "the nation of many nations," as Walt Whitman said. And that has formed a society that, at its heart, requires a certain amount of respect for things different. When differences are the norm, the need to protect that diversity is precisely what unites us. It's in the best interests of all.

Tolerance is a fundamental value in a multiethnic, multiracial, and multicultural society. It's the only way so many distinct people can live together. In its best examples, the United States doesn't define you by the language you speak or by your ethnic or racial origin. This is a nation of many races, ethnicities, and languages. And the U.S. defines itself by its values: its tolerance for diversity, its acceptance of immigrants, and its progressive drive. This is the place that both invented foreigners and made them its own.

In truth, the United States has historically been very generous with immigrants like myself. And that might upset some people. They might ask me how I can make such a statement after spending the past twenty years denouncing discrimination against undocumented immigrants and the mistreatment of immigrants in general throughout the United States.

Well, the two things are happening simultaneously. The U.S. has a sort of schizophrenia when it comes to immigration. Let me explain. On the one hand, every year it accepts hundreds of thousands of legal immigrants. But on the other hand, in its most conservative cities and communities, anti-immigrant political movements crop up, seeking to break with this great American tradition.

The United States—the world's only superpower, for now at least—needs to find a way to stop persecuting its most vulnerable inhabitants. It's an unjustifiable contradiction to have millions of immigrants living in fear in the land of liberty.

⌐ The United States—the world's only superpower, for now at least—needs to find a way to stop persecuting its most vulnerable inhabitants. It's an unjustifiable contradiction to have millions of immigrants living in fear in the land of liberty.

Ultimately, I believe—based on my own experience—that the United States will defend and honor that marvelous tradition of opening its doors to people from all over the globe looking for the opportunity to have a better life or seeking a refuge from political persecution.

Here there is a very tight relationship between effort and results. For those who work hard, things generally turn out for the better. And it's not that I have an overly optimistic vision of American society. It's a fact. Here I have seen Latin American poor rise from the humblest of roots to buy their own houses, and I've seen taco cart vendors and garbage collectors become millionaires.

In the United States—despite the wars and the ghosts—you can reinvent yourself. I know many more people here who have met with success than those who have failed to make it. I'm talking about success in its most basic definition: a safe place to live, a decent job, a school for your kids to attend, medical care, and—above all—the freedom to do and say what you want.

I know people who work much more than eight-hour days in San Salvador, Guatemala City, Oaxaca, and Medellín, and yet they still end up dying desperately poor. In places like those, the relationship between effort and results has been shattered. Just imagine how the future might look to a young man or woman from Chiapas or Bogotá who has just finished high school or even college only to discover that—despite the degree—there are no good jobs for them or their classmates.

I can't blame these young folks for starting to look to the north. I did the same thing. For a young Latin American kid, it's incredibly frustrating to know that there are still racial and economic barriers that not even a top-tier education can break down.

Children, you have to be so grateful to be here.

Latin America has some of the greatest inequity in the world. You two have seen it for yourselves whenever we go visit your grandmother and your cousins. An appalling distribution of wealth has the top ten wealthiest percent of the population raking in fifty percent of the gross earnings. That's why Latin America is currently walking in two different directions: making the rich richer while increasing the number of poverty-stricken people. This isn't a good thing.

And so Latin America continues to be the land of monopolies and oligarchs, where the few help themselves to the largest slices of the pie. And as long as that party isn't open to everyone, the people are going to continue looking and moving north. Latin America's top export is its best workers.

I have to admit that, from time to time, I feel a bit guilty for having left, for having realized that there were better opportunities for me here in the United States than there are for some of my friends and family in Mexico. It's inevitable. I'm still connected to the country of my birth and childhood. I also ask myself if leaving was the right thing to do. I didn't want to—I couldn't!—wait for Mexico to change and open up new possibilities for me. I was on the move, and the country wasn't moving nearly as fast as me. Those were different times, and they're why I left.

Even so, I feel a good bit of responsibility for what happens there. I feel obliged to contribute to the country and to the people I left behind. In that way, at least, it's as if I haven't really gone after all. I check the Latin American news obsessively. And often I'm even better informed about the goings-on there than I am about the United States. It's like living in two different parts of the world at the same time.

I still constantly think about going back. There's always that temptation, the feeling that return is possible, the hope that everything back home will be better now. Till you realize that the achievements you've made on this side of the border wouldn't be possible back there. And the illusion of return bursts like a bubble.

People naturally prefer to live in an already established society rather than one that is still being built. Those of us from Mexico who came to the U.S. didn't believe the politicians who promised a new government free of corruption and nepotism. We didn't have the patience to wait for better teachers to appear in our public schools. We weren't willing to risk having a child kidnapped by a narcogangster, or have our biweekly paycheck stolen at gunpoint by a police officer. We don't believe everything they put on TV. We don't wait for raises that we never see, or jobs that are never offered. We place our bets on the present, not on the future.

Have you noticed that the politicians in this country are almost always discussing the future and not the past? I come from a part of the world where getting bogged down in the past is a five-hundred-year-old tradition. But here even friends and family at funerals talk about overcoming the pain and moving on. To a foreigner, this seems like a rather strange approach, but it takes action in order to move ahead.

Of course, I don't want to paint a distorted picture of the United States. As I'm writing this letter, the nation is engaged in an unnecessary war in Iraq. Tens of thousands are dead, the majority of whom were innocent civilians. The reputation of the U.S. government has taken a severe hit all over the globe. But let me make this point: The United States is not identified by its president. And that's one of the amazing things about this country. It's defined by so much more than the decisions made by one man in an oval office in a white house. Fortunately.

∽ **And that's one of the amazing things about this country. It's defined by so much more than the decisions made by one man in an oval office in a white house.**

I covered the horrible terrorist attacks of September 11, 2001. Since all flights had been grounded indefinitely, the station drove me from Miami to New York to bear witness to what had occurred. And let me assure you that during those days, the rest of the world was with the United States. We all felt like Americans. But that international goodwill evaporated under the heat of a war being waged under false pretenses and against an enemy who'd had nothing to do with the terrorist attacks. Nevertheless, this is a country that knows how to change its course. Its system of checks and balances is designed to correct abuses of power. And this war, I hope, won't be the exception to that rule.

At the moment, we're living during turbulent times. So much so that you might look nostalgically upon the controlled tension of the cold war. But the international situation is very fluid. Terrorism will be part of our lives now, until we find some sort of structure under which we can live peacefully with extremely different cultures and ideologies. We need an international order that fosters contact among contrary systems of belief and eliminates the desire to destroy. And we're still quite far from achieving that. Difficult times are ahead.

War isn't the only thing that worries me about the United States. I know of few other countries in which religion is so tangled up with politics. That doesn't promote a healthy democracy. Neither is the arrogant use of power in a unipolar planet. In an age when terrorism can victimize us anywhere on the globe, it is important to form new alliances, not new disputes. Cooperating instead of imposing.

The United States can and should project those same democratic principles to the world—above all, respect for diversity and differences—which have done us so much good here at home. In the defense of human rights just as in the protection of the global environment. But recently these things have been lost.

There is no logic to a democracy that abuses its power abroad. However, don't get me wrong. Pointing out this country's errors and suggesting new pathways is a part of loving and respecting it. This perspective is just one of the things that we immigrants bring with us. I've learned that here. It is, after all, the country I chose for my family, and the country that has chosen us.

Sometimes I feel that I've found the perfect equilibrium here in the United States—a much different country than the one that I first met some twenty-five years ago. It's becoming so Latin Americanized that I'm constantly feeling more and more at home, and the rest of Latin America is becoming Americanized. And I'm sitting right in the middle, between the two parent nations. I'm always home.

In order to live a more or less healthy life, you have to remember three things: who you are, what interests you, and where you are from. And I'm from my home—the house I grew up in, where I slept, ate, played, shared with my siblings, and where I saw my parents every day.

I dream about it a lot. But sometimes the dreams are a bit different. Actually, there are a thousand different variations on the same theme. Now the backyard is encircled by red walls and covered with a log roof from which bougainvilleas hang. But the original house wasn't like that. There was no red wall and no bougainvilleas.

Different, yes, but deep down I know it's the same house. I know it better than any other, better than the one I'm living in now. And it's been over two decades since I've even laid eyes on it. The memory of that house gives me a sense of tranquility, security, and peace. It's where I'm from.

In the United States, on the other hand, I've moved so many times—I stopped counting at ten—that I have no special sense of attachment. I'm not tied to any of those places. And I ask myself if the same thing has happened to the two of you. Will you feel the same sense of security that I get from being from one particular place? I'm from that house. But you, where are you two from? Where do you feel the happiest? Which house do you dream about?

You come from many places. Paola, you are American, Latin American, and European. Nico, you're as Caribbean as you are Mexican and American. And after all, this gives you a much more global and tolerant view of life than the majority of people your age. It can be a great driving force in life. But I also occasionally ask myself if you'll ever feel adrift, anchorless, if you'll know where your home is.

And I hope that the answer is near to me.

But I also occasionally ask myself if you'll ever feel adrift, anchorless, if you'll know where your home is. And I hope that the answer is near to me.

With you. Always. Wherever that may be.
You know who

THE ARCHITECT WHO WANTED TO BE A MAGICIAN

⌣

To Jorge's grandchildren:

You never met him, Nico. You knew him for a few years, Paoli. And I knew him for almost forty. But in many respects, I didn't really know him at all. There are many things about your grandpa Jorge that I'd still like to know, and I'm trying to piece together the puzzle based on memories and questions I ask my mother.

I'd like to share with you this letter that I wrote to your grandfather years after his death, when the pain I felt was starting to subside. After reading it, perhaps you'll understand why I have so many unanswered questions about his life and the decisions he made. I'm also hoping that you come to understand me a little bit more, the way I'm hoping to understand him.

Here's the letter.

Hi Pa:

We just can't say good-bye.

It still hurts.

A lot.

I knew that when I went to live in the United States that something like this could happen. But I didn't even want to imagine that this would ever happen to us. Nobody is ever prepared for the death of his father. And I wasn't, Pa. I wouldn't want to be.

One night, while I was getting ready to do the news in Miami, I got a call from Mom in Mexico City. She told me that you were in the hospital again, and that things didn't look good. But I didn't detect a sense of urgency in her voice, no clear indication that something was about to happen, that you might pass away.

You know how Mom is. She says things so gently, not wanting us to worry, always thinking about others. And now I know that even then, she was trying to protect me. She didn't want me to start grieving ahead of time. The truth is that I didn't even suspect a thing. For years I'd been getting updates from her on the sudden changes in your health, so that particular conversation didn't seem abnormal in the least.

This time, though, something was different.

An hour or so later, Mom called again.

"Jorge, your dad just couldn't hang on any longer," she said slowly, her words interspersed with sobs. I wasn't expecting it, and I hadn't heard her very well, either. The mind works in mysterious ways, doesn't it? Things we don't want to hear never seem to register with us.

"What?" I asked, raising my voice. "He died?" That's how I said it. Bluntly. I couldn't believe it. Just a few minutes ago, you were alive, stable, safe in a hospital bed.

"Yes, son, he's gone," Mom managed to say.

My body went numb and I felt all my energy escaping through my feet. I don't know quite how to describe it; I suddenly felt empty inside, as if my bones were rubbery and I had no support.

We stayed there, Mom and I, crying over the phone. What a pathetic scene. And what a desperate situation: You had just died, and there I was, sitting in an office thousands of miles away, crying. I couldn't forgive myself for being so far away. I should have been there with you, but I wasn't.

And then I did something completely irrational.

I told my colleagues at work that something had happened, then I immediately followed that announcement by saying that I would still be doing the news that night. It was total denial. I didn't want to accept the fact that you were dead. I wanted life to keep on going just as it had been. And so—just like I said I would—I got back to editing that night's scripts.

My colleagues—who had become like extended family members and were accustomed to sharing the most personal and incredible things in the editing room—embraced me and insisted that I go home for the day. But I wouldn't listen. I simply ignored them. "I can do the news," I said. "Don't worry, I can do it." And that's how it was until my producer came up to me and gently yet firmly ordered me home for the day. I'll always be thankful to him. I just wasn't thinking clearly.

I cried all the way back to the house. I was crushed. But I still had to make all the arrangements to fly back to Mexico and pack my bags. Can you imagine me doing that, Pa?

At that moment, all I really wanted to do was lie down in bed and disappear.

At the funeral, I thought that it was my job to be the man

of the family and I unconsciously assumed that role. I figured that was what you would have wanted me to be. And I think you would have done the same thing: be in control. It was so difficult to tamp down my emotions, to be strong for the family. The truth is that my siblings and our mother had the hardest job of all. They were with you until the end.

And I'll admit something else to you. I didn't dare to look at you in the coffin. I preferred remembering you in life.

Of course, I knew that you were very sick. Still, though, I got some encouragement (and a few false hopes) when your doctor gave you permission to fly to Miami a few months before your death. I thought it was a sign that things were getting better. But that wasn't it. The doctor knew that you didn't have much time left, and he wisely allowed you to use it however you wanted to. He was a kind man, your doctor. He always looked at someone as a person first and a patient second.

I think we had a good time in Miami, don't you? We didn't overextend ourselves: just a couple of dinners out, chats at home, a little walk through the mall, and nights in front of the television. But what I remember most about that—your last visit—was how you'd changed. Nothing upset you, nothing bothered you, and you seemed to agree with just about everything.

When we were kids, you were oftentimes angry or upset and you almost always said no. But I don't think that was your true nature. I think that's how a father has to act sometimes. It's part of his role. Now I know that deep down you were a more tolerant, less controlling, more caring person than what you let on.

⌁ **Now I know that deep down you were a more tolerant, less controlling, more caring person than what you let on.**

Fathers of your generation are different. I think that we've reacted against the strictness and sternness with which parents of your generation raised us. At times, we've gone to the other extreme: You rarely played with your children, while we do all the time; you kept your distance and imposed your authority, while we do not; and you believed that consenting and giving in to your children would weaken them, whereas we do not. We try to be as accessible as possible to our children. Fathers of your generation didn't always.

You were always working or doing something. Always. You didn't know how to relax. I've never met anybody else who had such a hard time taking time off. It's almost as if you had some sort of great, internal sense of unrest that always drove you to action.

Now, as a father myself, I understand that your primary concern was providing for your family. Man, feeding five children, paying for private school, clothes, the occasional vacation or dinner out . . . that couldn't have been easy, right? I understand. It's why I didn't see much of you. You'd leave for work very early in the morning and return home just before we went to bed. For a while, you even had to work half days on the weekend. Remember?

Now I can understand, whereas when I was a child, I couldn't. But I never complained that you weren't spending enough time with us. To be honest, I never thought it would even be possible. It just wasn't what dads did back in those days. Or, rather, that's what I believed. And it's what you believed, too. So we missed out on the little wrestling matches and other sorts of physical contact that I now know are normal between fathers and sons. We were a family of few hugs and few kisses.

We both missed out. We just didn't know. It's a shame.

But in exchange for that lack of camaraderie, you gave us a

strong sense of security and confidence. If we were near to you, nothing bad could ever happen to us. You were the strongest, the greatest, and the one who could solve any problem. You have no idea how excited I was whenever you came home—every year or two—with a new car, honking at us from the driveway. And I never got tired of showing it off to my friends. And your face behind the wheel was like a poster of joy and satisfaction. I recognized it: It was the face of a boy playing happily with his new toy.

My siblings and I would get in the car, jumping from seat to seat, honking the horn like you did—two rounds of three short blasts—and you were the proudest dad in all of Mexico. Later, you'd give us a ride through the suburbs. You'd roll down the windows and rest your elbow there, driving with one hand while we looked out of the back windows so all our friends could see us. Seat belts didn't exist in those days, so the backseat was a chaotic mixture of arms, legs, and little blond heads.

To us, you were "Pa," while everyone else called you "the architect." But there was a lot of the architect in the Pa. You were always perfectly dressed and well groomed, with a colorful modern tie and a splash of aftershave to go with your mustache and sideburns. Your cigarettes—always lit when we were kids—made you look vaguely like a Mexican Humphrey Bogart. And your blue eyes completed the portrait. "Ay, your dad is so handsome!" Aunt Avalos would say whenever she came over for dinner on the weekend. And Ma would just smile knowingly. Those were your best moments: when you were in control, when things were going well, and when nobody was questioning you.

At that moment—not before, not after—you were happy.

I watched you pretty closely . . . did you notice?

When you would take a quick siesta after eating and before

heading back to work, I'd sneak up to your room and spy on you. You'd lie down, interlace your fingers across your stomach, and shut your eyes. I watched as your hairy fingers (including the one where you wore your ring with the green stone set in it) would rise and fall with the rhythm of your breathing. I never could tell whether you were sleeping deeply, but I was amazed at how you would jump right up after exactly twenty minutes. It even surprised me just how quickly you woke up. You'd brush your teeth, comb your hair, and splash on some aftershave before giving me a kiss, your mustache brushing my face . . . then I'd scratch the spot while you checked the back of your shirt for wrinkles.

I was quite intrigued by your prematurely gray hair, your hairless calves, the shape of your arches, and the reddish moles on your chest and back. And after examining you, I'd run straight to the bathroom mirror to see how I compared with you. I wanted to be exactly the same, but I wasn't. My skin was much darker, I didn't have a single hair on my face, and my legs were thicker than yours, from so much running and soccer.

∿ **I was quite intrigued by your prematurely gray hair, your hairless calves, the shape of your arches, and the reddish moles on your chest and back. And after examining you, I'd run straight to the bathroom mirror to see how I compared with you.**

To me, you were Superman—a little inaccessible and impenetrable. We didn't talk much or spend much time together, alone, just you and me. but you were invincible. I admired you. To me, everything you did was good.

Until one fine day when—completely unexpectedly—you

agreed to play some soccer with me. Well, it's not like we were going to organize a full game; rather, you agreed to take some penalty kicks while I would mind the net. I remember it like it was yesterday: We were at my grandpa's house. You, as always, were wearing black shoes and gray trousers. Elegant.

I situated myself in front of a door, which would serve as the goal, you stepped back, got a running start, and . . . you missed. The ball, I mean. Then, not acknowledging your first attempt at all, you gave the ball a little toe poke—this time you did make contact—and I made an easy save. And that was it. Our game lasted for one single shot. And you went off to talk with the grown-ups, leaving me in tears there in front of the door/goal.

I never told you this, but I was incredibly disillusioned when I found out that you couldn't kick a soccer ball. This had broken the invincible picture that I had of you.

Still, though, I needed one more test. And after much pleading, you finally agreed to accept my invitation for a game of basketball. After all, you'd told us that you'd played on the team in high school and college. From what I saw, it was just unfounded. I don't know whether you hit a basket or not, but—in the end—it was clear that you were not much of an athlete. Strange, right? I was measuring you by my own yardstick of what was important to me. And at that time the things that were important to me were soccer and basketball. Period.

I also think that those were the first signs of my own sense of independence emerging during my preadolescent years. I doubt that even if you had scored a goal or hit a shot against me, I would have been convinced. I was looking for a way to mark my separation. I was asking you to be someone you weren't, and that was impossible. And from that point on, we started to clash.

〜 I was looking for a way to mark my separation. I was asking you to be someone you weren't, and that was impossible. And from that point on, we started to clash.

I no longer liked the way you turned down the hot chocolate Mom made because (a) it didn't have enough foam on top, (b) it wasn't hot enough, (c) there was too much whipped cream, or (d) you were just in a bad mood. And your household rules—not being able to watch TV, play in the living room, or jump on the beds after 8:30—began to bother me. Everything was no, no, no.

One time, I snuck up behind you while you were on the sofa reading the paper, and I popped a balloon right next to your head. It was supposed to be a prank. It turned out to be quite the opposite. Blood started coming out of your ear, and you had to go to the hospital. While I was waiting for you to come home, I was scared to death. There would be some sort of punishment, or—even worse—you'd be shouting at me, something that always left me petrified with fear. But when you did come home, you behaved very calmly and didn't even say a thing to me. Not a word. And therein lies the point. For me that incident was laden with symbolism. Your world just couldn't accept things that came from mine. It hurt you.

The image of invulnerability I had of you continued to crumble when you were diagnosed with a very rare, very serious cerebral condition that could have killed you if one of your blood vessels had ruptured. You underwent emergency surgery at the Mayo Clinic—one of the best in the world—and Mom asked me if I wanted to go up to Minnesota to be with you. The situation was grave. The doctors gave you little chance of surviving without some sort of brain damage, and Mom—who had been prevented from being with her own mother on the day that she died—wanted me to be there for the surgery. I was just a little kid at the time, but on that trip I felt an enormous responsibility fall on my shoulders. I'd never feel like a child again.

I put you through a lot during my teenage years. Being the oldest child, I wanted some extra privileges, but you wouldn't grant me them. My curfews for coming home at night or after a party were always an hour or two earlier than those of my friends. I'm sure all teenagers complain about these things, right? I wasn't the exception. What was going on was that you and I were feeling each other out.

In our family dynamic—and particularly in our relationship as father and son—we never learned how to discuss our differences in a calm, organized fashion. Everything was formal and superficial, as if we were a bunch of British stereotypes holding umbrellas and discussing the weather. We almost never had a deep, meaningful conversation about what separated us. And when we finally dared to break with this code, you gave orders and I complained. We clashed.

Once, at dinner, you brought up the subject of religion. Strange. I figure you wanted to know why I didn't go to Mass anymore. And just to bother you, I said that I didn't believe in God. Your eyes almost jumped out of their sockets, and your face twisted up in anger. Mom and my siblings fell silent. In reality, at that time I was very confused and conflicted about the idea of religion, and I wasn't sure whether I believed in God or not. But I knew that what I said would hurt you, and so I said it. Awful, right? I'm sorry.

The worst of all was that I got up from the table—I always sat to your right—and left the dining room. That would have been an excellent opportunity to openly discuss a serious subject. An open and frank discussion where I would listen to your thoughts and you would listen to mine would have bridged the lack of communication between us, something that had been growing wider and wider. But your anger and my sharp remarks put an abrupt end to our dinner and conversation. Nobody wanted dessert after that.

We didn't talk about sex, either. Well, there was one time . . . today, I'm actually moved by the talk that we had. You invited me to go to the downtown shopping area to buy who knows what, and for some reason, I agreed. We had very little contact, and we both felt the same sense of responsibility for that. Plus, deep down, it was something we both needed.

We got in the car and put on some of the American orchestra music that you liked and suddenly—without any lead-up—you informed me that I should let you know if I ever wanted to be with a woman. That was it. Just like that. I assumed that you were offering to take me to a prostitute, but you never made it that explicit.

"No, Pa," I said. I don't think I even thanked you for asking me.

I'm sure you must have really called upon some sort of strength (I don't know where it came from) before asking me that question. To me, what you were proposing was outrageous. I had yet to have sex, but I'd talked about it with my girlfriend at the time. And I know I didn't want to lose my virginity to a prostitute.

That brief moment was yet another lost opportunity. You don't know how much that hurts me. If you had told me about your first time, maybe I would have opened up and told you about my own plans. I don't know. It's a complicated subject. But since neither of us had so much as broached the subject, we both felt very uncomfortable discussing it. Honestly, though, thank you. It was so hard for you to open up and talk about things that were so important to us both.

It might comfort you to know that I had my first sex talk with Paola in a car also. A little like what you did with me. And I'm sure that poor Nicolás will undergo the same, insufferable Ramos experience. You invented it, and it has a certain logic to it: Inside of a moving car, there's nowhere to go, so there's nothing for you to do but sit and listen to your dad.

Thanks, Pa. For trying.

You were a very strict father, and I only had two options: either submit and accept what you were saying or rebel against it. And, much to your dismay, I preferred the latter.

That would have been unthinkable with your father. He never allowed anyone to question him. We never talked about it, but I wish so much that I could learn about how you behaved around your dad, why he scared you so much, and why you preferred lying to him instead of facing him. But you never told me.

Talking about my grandfather—about his hard, steely character, his sharp, almost sour authority, and about his life in which he worked his way out of poverty to attain a law degree and several properties—would have brought us both so much closer together.

⌇ **Talking about my grandfather—about his hard, steely character, his sharp, almost sour authority, and about his life in which he worked his way out of poverty to attain a law degree and several properties—would have brought us both so much closer together.**

But we never did. Maybe you thought that talking about him behind his back would be akin to some form of betrayal, even if you were talking with your son. It was as if he could always hear everything you said. And I don't think you were ever fully able to work your way out from under his control.

I was the one Grandpa Gilberto pampered the most. He always gave me more candies than he did my siblings, gave me more money on Sundays, and gave me the privilege—which he didn't offer to the others—of going with him to the Ramos Arizpe ranch where he cultivated walnuts, oranges, and avocados. But, like you, he preferred silence to intimacy. That made an impression on me, despite being showered with material tokens of affection.

I always felt that your relationship with your father was a very tense one. More fear than love. I got the impression—and it's a shame that we didn't talk about this earlier—that he forced you to study architecture. I guess because when I went and chose an academic career, you suggested that I consider the same four options that your father suggested to you: architecture, engineering, medicine, or law. Those were—for you and for him—the only legitimate, valid options.

Of course, when I told you that I wanted to major in communications, you immediately jumped up and said, "And what are you going to do with that?" "That" referred to any degree other than the ones approved by Grandpa Gilberto. It was around that time, I think, when I removed the "Gilberto" from my compound name, Jorge Gilberto. Two Gilbertos in the family—you and him—were enough. I didn't want to be the third, and I didn't want to be a lawyer, doctor, architect, or engineer, either. When Nicolás was born, I decided to break with the tradition of names passing from father to son. No more Gilbertos, and no more Jorges. I wanted my son to carve out his own path, and to have an appropriate, original name.

You know, I have this theory that you would have preferred

being a magician to being an architect. I'm sure the other kids would think I'm crazy. But I'll tell you why.

When you performed those little magic tricks for us kids and our friends, or when you would come home from the magic shop with a new trick, your eyes would shine with an intensity that was common to you. You were like a kid again yourself. Really! When you were performing magic tricks, you had the look of a child. There was wit and shock and joy in your eyes. But only when you were a magician.

Your most often performed trick was when you pretended to pull off one of your fingers. We knew it by heart, but you always managed to capture our attention with it. Sometimes it even annoyed us when you went to a friend's house and immediately they asked you to perform something for the kids. "Oh, God," my siblings and I would say, under our breath. "There goes Dad with another one of his stupid tricks." But it wasn't any trouble for you, and the kids loved it.

Pa, I really think that magic was your true calling, and that you should have said to hell with Grandpa Gilberto's suggestions. You would have been happier. You were a good architect. But you didn't have passion to go with your profession. Magic, on the other hand, was yours.

You liked making things disappear.

I'm sure that if you could have, you would have snapped your fingers and made all the family pressure to be something you didn't want to be vanish. I think that by trying to please your father you lost your own path. You ended up trying to do two things at once: make Grandpa happy while secretly living the life you wanted. And at any given moment, you had to lie in order to protect that double life. That was your mistake. I'm not judging you. I'm only looking at your breaking point.

You tried to sell the image of a perfect son to your father. But it was his idea of perfection. Not yours. Left to your own devices, you would have chosen other paths. Less strict, perhaps less profitable, but much closer to what you truly wanted for yourself.

❧ You tried to sell the image of a perfect son to your father. But it was his idea of perfection. Not yours. Left to your own devices, you would have chosen other paths. Less strict, perhaps less profitable, but much closer to what you truly wanted for yourself.

Despite the fact that you were really a handsome guy, your eyes always held a hint of sadness and sorrow. And it was only when you were joking around that your smile emerged, free of fear, wreathed by your well-trimmed black and gray mustache.

I know you were at peace with yourself.

But when you realized that, you had already made a number of permanent choices. There was no backtracking. Honestly, I really do picture you wondering about how to earn enough money to feed so many kids while at the same time paying for the little toys and gifts that people expected from you.

You spent your days doing things you didn't enjoy doing. I'm not surprised that you changed jobs so often. You were never happy at any one particular job because, deep down, you weren't happy with yourself. Forgive me for saying so. The constant bad moods were just another sign of your unhappiness. You argued with the baker, and any poor guy who cut you off in traffic was quickly awash in insults and honking. We saw all this as a strange combination of fear and laughter. We never knew when another round of shouting would break out, and that's why we stopped riding along with you in the car.

You weren't a very introspective person. And that made it all the more difficult to change your path in life. After all, how can someone change if they don't know where they're going, or if they can't bring themselves to ask for help?

I know you looked for support from outside of our family, but that still didn't give you peace. It was a distraction, not a cure. You struggled to be yourself, but you just could never quite get there.

You know what? I learned something very important from you. It might sound rather harsh, but I'm going to tell you anyway. I learned by opposing you. I believed in confronting you. I learned not to follow your path. I didn't want to be you. I learned, as Hesse's Sinclair did, to allow myself to give in to my "imagination and intuition that arose spontaneously from the first strokes, as though out of the paint and brush themselves," to do what spontaneously appears in me. I saw you so uncomfortable—so dissatisfied with life—that I ended up looking to do the opposite of what you did. I went about choosing my career based on what I wanted to do instead of what others wanted for me. And, above all, I decided to live my life according to my terms and desires, and not what others thought they should be.

I learned to be myself. And I owe that to you.

But what hurts me the most is that I didn't know you all that well. We barely allowed each other to scratch the surfaces of ourselves. I wanted to know why you were so angry all the time, why you always felt the need to be doing something, why you weren't able to enjoy the simple things in life: a chat, a walk, a soccer game on TV.

What did seem to relax you was watering the plants in the backyard of our house. You spent about an hour or so out there every weekend. I watched you through your bedroom window, wondering all the while about what you were thinking. But I never bothered to ask. It was stupid of me, I know. You know what I'm missing? That unique connection that is supposed to develop between a father and his firstborn son.

However, things between you and I got better when I came here to the United States, didn't they?

When we broke through that authority-based relationship, we started to get to know each other better. The great irony is that this happened while we were thousands of miles apart. You were no longer the person who once told me that as long as I lived under your roof, I had to do what you said. And I was no longer the young rebel whose behavior seemed motivated only by a need to make things harder.

We let down our guard.

When I went back to visit you in Mexico City, you greeted me with so much affection and even with some gestures of appreciation—a long embrace, a sincere question about how my new life was going, a comment about how different I looked—that you'd never showed me before. Something was changing, and it was very, very sweet. I went shopping with you, we listened to some music in your car—the same as always, of course—and we even took a fascinating and wonderful trip through Greece, Egypt, and Israel.

Remember how nervous we were there, changing money on Cairo's black market? And the plane that swept across the desert, from the Egyptian capital to Tel Aviv? And the ship that took us to Crete, where we got tossed around like rag dolls during an overnight storm?

It was great getting my father back.

And I know that you felt the same way. Finally you could hug me, and—even though you didn't say it—you liked having me near. Mom says that you were very proud of me. You never told me that, but I could tell.

You were hit hard by each of your two heart attacks. And your physical limitations opened up an honest, emotional door. It wasn't that you were conscious of your own mortality; rather, it helped you to seek out company and support. After one of your hospital stays, your legs had become very slender and dry. And I rubbed you down with moisturizer as carefully and as gently as I could. It was the first time you ever let me touch you and take care of you in such a way. You thanked me a lot for that massage. The roles were being reversed.

We were also partners in crime when it came to a particular treat: rich, buttery cookies. Every time I went to Mexico, I would bring along several cartons of Pepperidge Farm Chessmen Cookies. You loved them. You used to hide them away like a treasure so my siblings and I couldn't find them. Pa, you're not going to believe this, but I still like them—especially with a pat of butter on top—and they still remind me of you.

Another one of our great joys was made possible, thanks to technology. One fine day you discovered that you could watch my news broadcasts from America right there in Mexico City via cable. So in that way, we had ourselves a nightly connection. Sometimes, remembering your affinity for flashy ties, I'd wear one in your honor. "Heck of a tie you wore tonight!" you told me over the phone after one such broadcast. (By the way, did I ever tell you that when I moved to the U.S., I helped myself to a few of your favorite ties? The one with the black and white stripes lasted until just recently.)

Most of the time you spent watching TV, you weren't paying attention to the news. You were watching me. Whenever I would ask you if you had seen this or that interview, you'd simply say that you didn't know, that you just wanted to see me. And so, even at a distance, you were with me, and I was with you.

Once again, we were accomplices. I knew that you were watching me, and you knew that I knew. Nobody else did. Except maybe Mom . . . though she would have let the two of us at least think we were the only ones sharing the secret. What a strange way of showing that you love someone: watching TV. But it worked for us.

I don't know why we never had very profound conversations, why we never talked about the things I'm writing here in this letter. Maybe you didn't want to force the fragile equilibrium that we'd worked so hard to establish. You seemed to prefer that relationship—cordial and caring, if incomplete—to running the risk of anger, misunderstandings, or a falling-out. But finally we had connected, and I wasn't about to lose it. Not again.

We had found our peace, right, Pa? I feel that, in the end, we were at least able to do that. That's why I can smile calmly whenever something happens to remind me of you.

As a kid, I don't remember you ever saying any of the things I wanted you to say to me. And I didn't tell you what you needed to hear, either. But after our reacquaintance, we got a second chance to talk. The first few times were tough. We had to break through the Ramos shell. After that, it began to feel more normal. That's how it should always have been.

And two people who lost some of the most from your quick exit were my kids. Paola was luckier—when you visited us, she liked to snuggle in bed between you and Mom—and you'll never know how much she cried the day I told her you had died. She cried and cried, and she just couldn't understand how someone could be there one minute and be gone in the next. I sat there hugging her for several minutes until she calmed down. Then she asked me if you had gone up to heaven with the stars, and I said yes. What else could I have said? It was the first time I'd had to face something like that.

And with Nico, you spent some fun times watching soccer on TV. You have no idea how great he's playing. He takes free kicks like Beckham; it's such a spectacle to watch him play. I can almost imagine you there, on the sidelines, watching him every Saturday in the youth championship league. I was a good soccer player, but Nico is great. He says he wants to play in the World Cup one day, and I (you can imagine) am just thrilled. We're starting to see what he wants to do with his life and his powerful, athletic legs.

You know what? I've thought a lot about your dying so young. Only sixty-three years old. Just think what could have been, Pa. While I was going through some of your old papers, I found your death certificate. I don't remember ever having seen it before. It's a photocopy, and I can barely read it. Under the heading "Cause of Death" it reads "Insufficient cardiac retraction, acute myocardial infarction, and arteriosclerosis." Which must refer to all those cigarettes, and your daily breakfast of eggs, bacon, buttered bread, and hot chocolate. The doctor told us your veins and arteries looked like they were made out of cardboard. Could that be true? I never remember you ever exercising. Actually, I don't even remember you owning a pair of tennis shoes. One day we went to the Acapulco beach, and you came out wearing your black work shoes and dark socks and with your trunks on under your wool trousers. My siblings and I got quite a laugh out of that. Sartorially speaking, leisure did not come easy to you.

After you died, everyone in the family had a checkup with the cardiologist. But I'm still trying to figure out how many more years you might have had if you had smoked a few less cigarettes.

We just didn't know then how bad it was. Finally accepting your death took a lot out of me, you know? And the hardest part of all was the emptiness. That terrible, aching hole. It was knowing that you weren't going to pick up the phone ever again, or watch one of my news broadcasts, or give off that scent of tobacco and aftershave.

I dragged that emptiness with me for a long time. Until one good day when I had the chance to interview the Chilean writer Isabel Allende. She had just lost her daughter Paula to a terrible disease, and was promoting her last book. By one of those strange coincidences, Mom was in Miami and I invited her to the interview. The two of them clicked right from the start. It was quite impressive, really. And the three of us commiserated with the pain of losing a dearly loved family member.

A few weeks after the interview, I got a wonderful card from Isabel. In it she'd written the best advice I've ever received. She said that "the most beloved dead never completely go . . . your father is within you now, you carry his memory, his genes, and in the many mannerisms you now have, though they once belonged to him."

That, Pa, changed everything.

All of a sudden, I began finding you in myself. Do you know that I yawn just like you would? And that I try to catch mosquitoes in the air like you did? The color of my belly and my fingernails is the same as yours was, as are the arches in my feet. We both get chilled to the bone in the slightest breeze. We're both very sentimental, though we hide it underneath a layer of seriousness. We listen to loud music in the car. And we both like to cuddle, though we'd never say it or ask for it. We're just a couple of hidden children.

⌐ All of a sudden, I began finding you in myself. Do you know
that I yawn just like you would? And that I try to catch
mosquitoes in the air like you did? The color of my belly
and my fingernails is the same as yours was, as are the
arches in my feet.

Every time I see something of yours in me—especially if it's
right on—it makes me happy. That heavy sadness I used to as-
sociate with your memory is over and done with. Now thinking
of you is fun; it's something to celebrate. I see you everywhere,
which means you are with me every single day.

I know that you believed that, after death, we will all reunite
in heaven. Then again, maybe heaven is here and now. Maybe
somehow I'm carrying you inside of myself, and maybe Nicolás
has a little piece of you, too. I was shocked the other day when I
saw him yawning just like the two of us. There he was, his mouth
wide open, making that unmistakable guttural noise. "You yawn
just like your grandpa Jorge," I told him, and when I hug him, it's
as if—somehow—I'm hugging you as well. Strange, right? But
sweet nonetheless.

At the beginning of this letter, I said that I had suffered a lot
for not being able to say good-bye to you. But now that I think
about it, we did make our farewells.

A couple of weeks before you died, I went to visit you in your
new apartment in Mexico City. It was a bit cold outside, and you
were wearing a beautiful wool sweater. It was a little itchy. We
talked about what we always talk about, which is to say, nothing
important, and then I gave you a hug and a kiss and said good-
bye. I walked toward the door before turning around to look
at you. I don't know why, but I just couldn't go. Something had

stopped me. I saw your blue eyes, a bit sadder than normal, and I walked back to you and gave you another hug. This time it was long, tight, cheek to cheek, and I could feel the emotion in your breathing. We just couldn't let go.

That was our final embrace, Pa. It was our farewell.

WHERE I KEEP MY SECRETS

⌁

One of the secrets of life is that all that is really
worth the doing is what we do for others.

—LEWIS CARROLL

My children:

I keep secrets hidden everywhere. And here I'm going to tell
you how to find them.

Some things are uniquely mine. And one of these is that I
play classical guitar. It's an open secret—though I've quite literally kept it in a closet. The closet in my office, to be precise.

I've neglected my guitar. Just like when I was taking lessons
as a kid. As a matter of fact, it's a mystery as to how it's managed
to last this long without breaking. It's a good Michoacána guitar.
And you're not going to believe this, but the strings have never
snapped. Not one of the six.

That guitar has accompanied me through every step of my
American adventure. It came to Los Angeles with me some
twenty-odd years ago, and it's still right there, looking at me,

silent, desperately wanting to vibrate again, to make sounds. Always waiting for a moment of desperation or nostalgia when I'll pick it up and bring it back to life. An unplayed guitar is an opportunity lost—a singer without a voice. But she—my guitar, that is—knows that one day I'll be back. She's my stringed Penélope.

It all began with a misunderstanding.

When I was around twelve years old, I told my dad that I wanted to learn to play the guitar. Actually, what I should have said was that I wanted to be a rock star; I wanted to play stadium shows and jump around onstage waving my arms and belting out lyrics. I loved The Beatles—or *Los Bítles,* as they said in Mexico—and they had a song, "Michelle," which I wanted to learn to play.

The fact is that my dad knew someone who gave guitar lessons at the local YMCA, so he took me. My teacher, Oscar Cué, was no rocker. He had long hair all right, but he was a master of the classical guitar. It sure didn't sound like The Beatles, but it was certainly better than nothing. And it was there, between the strings, that I discovered something: playing the guitar relaxed me, transported me into an alternative universe.

See if you can picture your father like this: Instead of playing rock riffs on an electric guitar, I was playing Spanish compositions dating back to 1580—one of which was titled "Look After My Cows," which I was always hesitant to admit to anyone listening to me—and works by Johann Sebastian Bach, Puccini, and Francisco Tarrega. Of course, when I went to parties and my friends wanted to hear me play, it was no fandango. They would say, "Ah, yes, you play so beautifully," listen for a few minutes just to be polite, and then go off to dance. For my part, I'd put down the guitar and go off in search of some rock-and-roll.

But the guitar opened many doors to me. The first time I ever appeared on TV was playing in a national talent show. I was the only kid participating, and I was quickly eliminated. But I didn't care. I overcame my nerves and continued to practice. At sixteen, I gave my first concert. I have here in front of me the program from that show, and my picture appears on it: I'm looking very serious (weird, right?) in a plain gray suit, one of my dad's ties, and a swatch of hair that almost covered up my eyes.

I think I gave one more performance and then stopped taking classes. In reality, I didn't have a good musical ear, and I decided I'd rather devote my time to school. For me, the guitar just wasn't the right form of expression. But over eight years of practice have left their permanent mark on me.

I no longer have calluses on the tips of my fingers, but I do still keep my fingernails trimmed very short. It might be hard to believe, but the piece I played on that TV show—Robert de Visee's Allemande Courante Sarabande Suite No. 3 in D Minor—is the only thing I remember in its entirety. Of the rest, all I have left are little bits here and there.

But that was enough for me to escape through the strings.

Playing the guitar helps me live in peace. I actually don't play very much, but the little that I do relaxes me. With those first few chords, I feel the instrument vibrating against my legs, my stomach, my chest. It's the feeling you get right before a kiss. The best is when nobody is there to hear me, when it doesn't matter if I hit the wrong note . . . when I'm alone with the guitar, she almost becomes a person herself. We chat, we fight, we push each other, we pull each other, we love each other.

⌒ With those first few chords, I feel the instrument vibrating against my legs, my stomach, my chest. It's the feeling you

get right before a kiss. The best is when nobody is there to hear me, when it doesn't matter if I hit the wrong note . . . when I'm alone with the guitar, she almost becomes a person herself. We chat, we fight, we push each other, we pull each other, we love each other.

The guitar doesn't have the force of the violin or the volume of the trombone or the drums, but on the other hand it does have that smoothness that flows so well with the rhythm of the heart. The sound of the guitar massages me from within. Watching one of her strings vibrating up close is almost hypnotizing: a long, oval shape that eventually ends up, exhausted, as a straight line.

The music on my iPod is a mixture of modern guitar music, ranging from Christopher Parkening, Sting, Maná, Shakira, Ana Torroja, Dido, Damien Rice, Serrat, Julieta Venegas, Lu, Bosé, Reyli, U2, and Bob Marley, among others.

Sometimes I go running with that little white instrument. That's my other form of escape, of reducing stress. It's something I also picked up during my teenage years, back when I was fixing to become an Olympic athlete. I think you know the story, but let me start from the beginning.

I run. Fast. I always have. And one time I even convinced an official of the Mexican Olympic Committee to let me train to compete as a track and field athlete in the Summer Games. I don't know how I did it. But the day after I applied (it was more a supplication than an application) I was running laps at the official Mexican athletic training compound.

I was intrigued by the high jump, but since I couldn't even clear the bar at five feet nine inches, my future in that event was cut short. From there, I went on to try the four-hundred-meter intermediate hurdles. And that made it clear to everyone—including my coach—that running was my thing. Unfortunately, though, I ended up with a stress fracture in my back that ended my Olympic aspirations.

That fracture, just above my hips, was the first symptom of what I later discovered to be a malformed spinal column. It took me completely by surprise. If I hadn't wanted to compete in the Olympics, it wouldn't have mattered. But a series of medical tests and scans determined that my vertebrae hadn't been developing properly since birth, and that—if I wanted to continue to pursue my Olympic dream—I would have to undergo a dangerous operation. And it wasn't an easy choice: If the operation went wrong, I could be left paralyzed, and even if it went well, my range of motion could still be restricted so much that I wouldn't be able to resume training.

After several weeks of worry and consultations with my parents, I decided not to have the surgery, to return to a normal life, and to hang up my spikes and my Olympic dreams. It was the first time in my life that I cried and cried uncontrollably. My childhood was filled with dreams, and now my most beloved would never come true.

⌐ **After several weeks of worry and consultations with my parents, I decided not to have the surgery, to return to a normal life, and to hang up my spikes and my Olympic dreams. It was the first time in my life that I cried and cried uncontrollably.**

I'd have to reinvent myself.

My after-school time, which had been dedicated to training,

was now more like torture. I didn't know what to do. I could play some guitar, but after a couple of hours I was agitated again. I needed to do something physical, something that would burn off some of my extra energy. My legs were itching to move. My teenage body was about to explode. So, against the doctors' orders, I started running again.

Of course, the runs weren't the rigorous workouts that I had been doing with the pre-Olympic team; they were just long runs through my neighborhood. I would run until I was tired, until my mental stresses had returned to some sort of balance. I felt better after running. Life could go on. I was always careful to run on soft surfaces and trails, so as not to aggravate my back condition. And after a few months, the pain in my back was gone. I literally ran away from my problems.

Even better: A few minutes into a run, I could think with greater clarity than at any other time during the day. And after several months of running, I learned to enter into that state of concentration—what athletes call "the zone"—and I felt as if I were floating. When my body reached that point of absolute fluidity and harmony, pain and fatigue melted away. And my objective was to extend it as much as possible. It was almost like being in a state of hypnosis. A pure runner's high. Occasionally a car, a dog, a noise, or a stray thought would break my concentration. But that sense of being complete—of not needing anything else—was unique.

It's the best thing I learned from running.

I couldn't go to the Olympics, but I had found a way of living a better life without so much stress. I never used drugs to escape from my reality; all I needed was a pair of running shoes and a road. That was where I found my solutions.

Another thing I learned from all the time I spent training was that you should always run through the finish line. Stopping before you reach the goal or even slowing your rhythm can change everything, and change you from a winner into a loser.

> ⌁ Another thing I learned from all the time I spent training was that you should always run through the finish line. Stopping before you reach the goal or even slowing your rhythm can change everything, and change you from a winner into a loser.

To this day, whenever I feel stressed out about this or that problem, I go for a run. The most difficult moments of my life are either preceded or followed by a good run. I always feel better and more clearheaded after doing so.

It's the secret I found in my feet.

Other secrets I found in books.

Reading is a solitary activity. Have you ever noticed a sort of sadness or melancholy in someone reading? At that moment, he prefers to be by himself. He's choosing the internal over the external. There is something of a contained intensity in the act of reading. Why do we do it? Because through reading we can immerse ourselves in new worlds, sink into other people's lives, recover deeply hidden secrets, witness things we never could have imagined on our own. Reading unlocks places, circumstances, and feelings that—before you opened the book—were unknown. And, above all, it connects you: with yourself, with the author, with the characters, with other times or with things that frighten or thrill you. We read because, with a book in hand, we are others.

> ⌁ Reading unlocks places, circumstances, and feelings that— before you opened the book—were unknown. And, above

all, it connects you: with yourself, with the author, with the characters, with other times or with things that frighten or thrill you. We read because, with a book in hand, we are others.

There are books in my life that are akin to best friends. *Demian, Ulysses,* and *Paula* have been with me as long as my great friends. The way in which Hermann Hesse begins his novel *Demian* always seemed brutal and defiant to me. The first time I read it, when I was sixteen or seventeen years old, it really shook me up. "Unquestionably I belonged to the realm of light and righteousness; I was my parents' child. But in whichever direction I turned I perceived the other world, and I lived within that other world as well . . ." I also wanted to live that way: rebelling against my family, my school, my society, my country, and motivated only by my desires and restlessness. But to me it seemed—as it did to Demian—next to impossible.

I took that opening as a manifesto, as a declaration of war. And even though it's rooted in youth, I still reread it from time to time, just to keep me alert. To advance, you have to rebel. And sometimes the hardest thing to do is to rebel against the comfort and mediocrity of our own lives. That's why I hold *Demian* as a sort of amulet.

That search for your own identity—which I painfully endured through the books of Erich Fromm, Erik Erikson, and even Ortega y Gasset—has its foundations in Hesse's *Demian.* That was the direction I needed, and I hadn't found it anywhere else. I didn't have any answers to the most common vital questions: Who am I? Why am I here? And it caused me much distress.

The answers came to me, page by page, in books.

Being and loving are the only important things. A bit melodramatic, don't you think? During those times in which we can find no answers—when you don't know who you are, when you wonder whether your life has any meaning to it—the message of being and loving was the answer to all my doubts. It calmed me considerably. Yes, they were (for lack of a better term) boxed answers, but, bit by bit, they began to make sense. It was a way of being authentic and connecting myself to others.

In those days, before I went off to college, there was an Argentine singer named Nacha Guevara who set poems by Uruguay's Mario Benedetti to music. I went to see her a number of times, and I was always impressed by the presence she had onstage. I understand that she's still out there, scandalizing audiences across Argentina. Marvelous! In fact, it's thanks to Nacha that I started to read Benedetti. And more than any of his novels, there is one poem in particular that I've made into my own personal prayer:

> Don't stand there still
> Along the side of the road;
> Don't isolate joy,
> Don't love without hunger,
> Don't save yourself now . . .
> Don't ever
> Save yourself.

Books weren't truly important to me until I took my first class in literature with Miss Nora. Miss Nora was a revolutionary in disguise.

She built her reading list with unnerving and perturbing titles such as Hesse's *Steppenwolf* and Kafka's *The Metamorphosis*.

When Gregor Samsa woke up one morning from unsettling

dreams, he found himself changed in his bed into a monstrous vermin.

"What's happened to me?" he thought. It was no dream.

I was stuck by the gray, bureaucratic, self-contained universe of Kafka's creation. It reminded me of the dark world of Mexican politics from which I wanted to escape. I didn't want to feel like Gregor Samsa.

The next thing that the literary guerrilla Miss Nora led me to was Mario Vargas Llosa's *The City and the Dogs.* My school didn't have nearly as much torture and violence as the one in the Peruvian author's novel, but I did see something of his characters in the unconscious cruelty of some of my friends.

Nobody did anything to me in school because I was under the protection of Armando "El Perro" Lage, a strong, unconditional friend who was feared by the other students. Others weren't so lucky. We gave people the most obscene and denigrating nicknames—two friends were dubbed "El Sope" and "La Tostada," while others were simply unrepeatable—and our jokes weren't of the laughing sort.

Today, some forty years later, I still feel remorseful for what we did to another boy whose name I'd rather not mention. We had the lamentable habit of "depantsing" our weaker and more vulnerable classmates. In those days, I suppose that we found such things fun, but in reality it was a very cruel practice. It consisted of surrounding the unfortunate victim, pinning him to the ground, and literally pulling his pants off of him. It was as painful as it was humiliating.

Well, this poor guy happened to be wearing his twin sister's underwear when we depantsed him. We never found out why. I figure it was because all his shorts were dirty, and he'd decided he'd rather wear something clean, whatever it was. Who knows? But his shame was so great that he never returned to school. And the following year, his twin sister left as well. There was something about that situation that reminded me of *The City and the Dogs*.

I wouldn't read Marcel Proust until much later. There's no better title for a book than *In Search of Lost Time*. Every writer claws at his childhood. The process of remembering and reliving a simple sensation in the present—for Proust, it was the aroma of French *madeleines*—showed me a new way of examining my life.

Life does not simply evaporate with time; it can be brought back by a memory, a smell, or with the simple act of closing your eyes. It's a wonderful feeling to know that the past—or at least a part of it—can be recalled at will. For me, realizing that the past is hidden in present-day objects was a great discovery. Strangely enough, my dad also really liked those *madeleines*, which he called *rayaditos*. And I'm still eating them myself. It's one way I remember him.

In fact, I'd go so far as to say that all books are, at some level, attempts to recover lost time. "I came to Comala because I had been told that my father, a man named Pedro Páramo, lived there." That's how Juan Rulfo began his eponymous novella. And Gabriel García Márquez opens *One Hundred Years of Solitude* with "Many years later, as he faced the firing squad, Colonel Aureliano Buendía was to remember that distant afternoon when his father took him to discover ice."

Time is a constant theme throughout literature, but it was literature itself that helped me understand the nature of time, and—by extension—life itself. The things I found in books changed the way in which I perceived things in real life.

〜 Time is a constant theme throughout literature, but it was literature itself that helped me understand the nature of time, and—by extension—life itself. The things I found in books changed the way in which I perceived things in real life.

Reading García Márquez introduced me—happily—to a life orbited by both dreams and reality. And my frequent travels through Latin America proved that his words were the product of not only a prodigious sense of creativity but also of close and careful observations of reality. Before becoming a writer of fiction, García Márquez was a brilliant reporter and an extremely accurate witness.

I think I've read every one of his books. I admire his unequalled ability to select the precise word for expressing exactly what he wants to say. Nobody does it quite like him.

I prefer *The Autumn of the Patriarch* to his more famous *One Hundred Years of Solitude*. With infinite vulnerability, he paints the portrait of the political and military dictators who have governed our part of the world. What surprises me is that his keenly critical vision of such leaders does not include his friend Fidel Castro. There, he blinks.

How could one want democracy for everyone except for the Cuban people? Some time ago, he and I sat down to a long and fascinating breakfast in Los Cabos. Everything was off the record, and I will continue to respect that. But it was clear to me that García Márquez was not about to betray a friend in the waning years of his life, even if he had become a bloodthirsty tyrant.

Past and present confound, converge, and coexist.

Jorge Luis Borges once wrote, "The past is indestructible."

It's the one thing that we are powerless to change. We drag it along behind us. Forever. The years I spent at that school feel like yesterday.

⌐ Jorge Luis Borges once wrote, "The past is indestructible." It's the one thing that we are powerless to change. We drag it along behind us. Forever.

I have to admit that Borges confused me the first time I read him. I was lost in the labyrinths and mirrors of *The Aleph*. But from that book I learned that order and chaos flow together. There are no purities.

I always imagine Borges sitting down, a serious look on his face, one bad eye drifting away while he contemplated important things. What I never imagined was apologizing for being "one of those people that lived sensibly and prolifically each minute of his life," a poem often (though not definitively) attributed to Borges. But whomever the poet may be, the case he makes is this:

> *If I were able to live my life anew,*
> *In the next I would try to commit more errors . . .*
> *Take more vacations,*
> *Contemplate more sunsets . . .*
> *If I could go back I would try*
> *To have only good moments.*
> *Because if you didn't know, life is made only of them:*
> *Of moments. Don't lose the now.*

Moments. That's what it's all about. Pure moments.
Pramoedya Ananta Toer also wrote about the importance

of moments. I discovered her by chance, and I was particularly taken with *Mute Soliloquy: A Memoir* and *The Buru Quartet*, in which she addresses the many years she spent as a political prisoner in Indonesia and her childlike sensibility:

"There are many people who would prefer to forget or even erase from their lives certain events and experiences, the knots which—in the great net of experience—ultimately unite all people trapped in the same web of time."

Like anyone else, I occasionally like the idea of trying to erase certain events from my life. To hit the delete key and be done with someone who betrayed me, hurt me, or abused my confidence. But doing so would take a part of me with it. And I don't want to rewind time. First of all, because it's as ridiculous as it is impossible. And second, assimilating all those years has allowed me to use my experiences to enjoy life more and to avoid repeating the errors of my past. I live more calmly, conscientiously, and passionately now, in my fifties, than I did when I was in my twenties.

It might seem like I'm giving you homework, but actually I just want you to know that books, writers, ideas, and words have left their mark on me.

Hopscotch by Julio Cortázar was the first book that I approached as a game. Its unique ways of being read, jumping from chapter to chapter, was a complete surprise. In Cortázar's novels, life isn't linear. And when I came to the end of the book, I realized that our own lives are neither linear nor logical. It was the magic of La Maga, the novel's protagonist.

Contrary to García Márquez, the Mexican writers Carlos Fuentes and Octavio Paz do occasionally dare to denounce the abuse of power by rulers like Castro. I enjoy them more, however, when they focus their attention on Mexico. Mexico hurts

Fuentes and Paz. It hurts me, too. A lot. It hurts me because I would like it to be a productive country, free from the clutches of poverty and clear of the malevolent cloud that holds so many people down. It hurts that I had to leave. Then I reread an old book, and finally I was able to make sense of the Mexican mystery.

Paz's *The Labyrinth of Solitude* is the best portrait ever painted of what it means to be Mexican. Read, if you would, this little excerpt: "The Mexican . . . seems to me to be a person who shuts himself away to protect himself: his face is a mask and so is his smile."

Fuentes is one of those Mexicans who feel comfortable anywhere in the world, and who see no human issue as being foreign to them. He is a global Mexican. Or globally Mexican. And he has understood as few have that Mexico's main contribution to the world is its culture. "Mexico: her hands empty of bread but her head filled with dreams," he wrote in *Inés' Instinct*.

I've met them both, and ever since then I've understood that it is indeed possible to be from Mexico and of the world at the same time. What a wonderful gift, don't you think?

In his book *The Cosmic Race*, another Mexican writer, José Vanconcelos, showed me the power of mixing: "The ulterior goals of history [are] to attain the fusion of peoples and cultures." The mixing—*lo mestizo*—is stronger than the pure. So it should come as no surprise, then, that the most diverse nation on earth—the United States—is, for now, also the most powerful.

In the U.S., I got a much better understanding of the relationship between distant travels and your inner self. In order to find yourself, first you have to leave. But it was a very hard lesson to learn. I felt like Ulysses in Homer's *The Odyssey*, whose one and only desire was to return home after twenty years away.

In the end, I never did return home. Instead, I've found another, here, with the two of you. So you see, there are many books that have been my traveling companions on this one-way voyage. Others have caused me pain. *Paula* by Isabel Allende is one of these. My hands tremble every time I pick it up, even before I open it. I have no idea how Isabel could possibly write about her daughter's death. But she did, and now it's a book filled with love. It's the most tender—and terrible—conversation that a mother can have with her daughter.

At the end of this long list, I have to mention two extraordinary books that I wholeheartedly recommend. *Perfume* by Patrick Suskind allowed me to smell in a way that my poor nose doesn't. It's marvelous. And *The Shadow of the Wind* by Carlos Ruiz Zafón has to be one of the best narratives I've ever read. It brings me as close to the streets of Barcelona as I can get without physically walking down them.

The Italian journalist Oriana Fallaci opened my eyes to the possibility of confronting those in power and asking them questions. It's possible. Oriana could. And she did, in her book *Interview with History*.

"I do understand those who oppose power, who criticize power, who contest power, especially those who rebel against power imposed by brutality," she wrote in her prologue. "I have always looked on disobedience toward the oppressive as the only way to use the miracle of being born."

And I would like to do the same.

To ask.

Everything.

Those interviews with presidents, dictators, and the like were filled with hot sparks and courage. She dared to ask the questions that nobody else asked. Two women you've never met defined my career and made me into an inquisitive person.

This is another secret.

The Mexican writer Elena Poniatowska does much the same thing.

La Noche de Tlatelolco (translated into English as *Massacre in Mexico*) is the other book that drove me to become a reporter. Poniatowska, alone, with a tape recorder slung over her shoulder, saved the testimonies of those people who survived the worst massacre in modern Mexican history. Hundreds of students were shot and killed by the Mexican army on the night of October 12, 1968, in the Plaza of the Three Cultures, in the Tlatelolco section of Mexico City.

My copy of the book is almost forty years old. It's as tattered as the justice system itself in Mexico. And yet blood and indignation still pour from its pages. The book is at once beautiful and terrible. And it proves that a reporter can keep history alive until justice is finally served.

Her weapon? Questions.

"I'm the sort of person who is always full of questions. Maybe it's because I don't yet have the answers; maybe that's why I'm still asking questions and looking for answers as to why and for what are we here," she once said in an interview. "That's why I became a journalist, why I haven't stopped asking questions, because the five pillars of journalism—who, what, when, where, and how—are, for me, still unanswered."

Kids, you have to filter everything through these questions. Just like Elena and Oriana did. There is no such thing as a stupid question. And nothing is off limits. There are no questions that you can't ask. If you don't know something, ask. And if you think you do know something, ask again, and find out even more about it.

As you know, I've made being nosy and prying into a profession. I live to ask questions; it's what I'm paid to do. But this professional necessity has seeped into my personal life. I pry. All the time. Into everyone. So much so that people are occasionally offended.

And the two of you are no exception. I'll often subject you to a battery of questioning. I don't mean it in a nagging sort of way. I just honestly want to know about what's going on in your lives. For me, it's just part of loving you.

During the last few years, I've tried to cut down on my need to be asking so many questions, and now I'm trying to focus more on offering my own opinions and information. And I think I'm doing better. There's more balance. People seem more at ease around me. They don't feel like they're in an endless interrogation anymore.

Ultimately, he who asks the questions is the receiver, and he who responds is the giver. I've received a lot, and now I'm learning how to give. I try to be merciless when it comes to questioning myself. There's nothing harder than asking yourself every day if you're happy, if you're being honest, if you're contributing something valuable to this world, if you love the people you're with, and if you're doing what you most enjoy doing.

〜 **Ultimately, he who asks the questions is the receiver, and he who responds is the giver. I've received a lot, and now I'm learning how to give. I try to be merciless when it comes to questioning myself.**

It's hard, but asking these sorts of questions is the best way of getting to know yourself. Everything I do gets evaluated. I live through self-examination. I ask, therefore I am. And hopefully

I can take that information and turn it into something useful . . . which is where writing comes in. Another one of my little secrets.

For me, it's not the product that's important, it's the process. Pages emerging from the printer are like feelings being rolled out on paper. It's the juice I extract in order to relax my soul.

Of course, it would be much more romantic to speak in terms of pen, paper, and the written word. In reality, however, I write sitting at a computer. Kids: We are adapting to everything. In front of this monitor, I've cried all alone and I've laughed out loud like a madman. Alone. Writing has allowed me to bring out things that have been caught up in my throat and my stomach for a long time.

You would think that my work as a journalist would help me draw out—via TV broadcasts, radio commentaries, or newspaper columns—all my thoughts and feelings. But it doesn't quite work like that. In fact, my thoughts and opinions are what I keep most closely guarded at work. When you try to paint an objective version of reality, it's best to keep your own point of view to yourself.

That's a big part of journalistic work. We stow away—actually, we swallow—our own feelings. And let me assure you, that sort of thing can cause ulcers, ruin relationships, send you to a therapist, or—in the worst of cases—to a bar. Unless you write.

I write so that I won't start to die from within. I write so that I can let out what gets caught up inside me every day. I write so that I don't drag around dead weight from year to year. I write as a form of escape, a form of therapy, a release, a discipline, a form of exercise, a plumber cleaning out a set of pipes. And it is, I admit, something I had to learn.

There are people who never write, and they live very well.

But I can't do that. Maybe I could if I were more expressive or extroverted. For me, there's just no better remedy than writing. So I write. And I write. And I write.

Time seems to accelerate when you write. Have you ever noticed that? Three hours can just fly right by. On the other hand, those same three hours—spent on a plane from Miami to New York or Mexico City—seem interminable. Writing has that ability to unite the exterior with the interior. Clocks and watches don't work right when you're writing; their minutes and seconds are for another universe.

Before, I would hide what I wrote. And again I'm not talking about articles or news reports. It was a sort of diary, a project through which I documented the early years of my life. After all, when we're young, we're pure promise. Later, in midlife, I began to share what I was writing . . . with just a few people. And now, as you can see with these letters, I think it's a waste to write without sharing your words with your friends. With age, if you've lived well and have little in the way of secrets and regrets, you realize that it's just not worth it to hide yourself. Why? Because, in the end, it's gone in a snap or in the blink of an eye.

That's why I write. And why I write to you. Why these letters are yours. I can't wait to give them to you. They're practically burning my hands. I write with urgency, as if time is running out on me. And I hope that when you read these letters, they'll cease to be mine and become yours.

I love you with all my heart, my feet,
My questions, my eyes, with everything

A LITTLE *BIT* ABOUT LOVE

To my supercalifragiloved children (even if that sounds stupid):

I spent weeks thinking about what to tell you about love, and I'm still basically stuck. No matter what I write here, I'm finding it impossible to describe to you what it means to love someone. You have to experience it yourself. And no matter how much I might want to, I just can't protect you from the pain caused by a broken heart. It's one of the hardest things to endure in your life.

I said this once, and so I'll offer it to you here, too.

When love strikes, it's impossible to hide it. Don't even try. Just let it flow. So it shows, so it's obvious, so everybody knows. But above all, let the person you love know. It's one of the greatest joys of being alive. More than anything else, love unites you to another person and makes you distinct.

〜 **When love strikes, it's impossible to hide it. Don't even try.
Just let it flow. So it shows, so it's obvious, so everybody
knows.**

When I was your age, Paoli, or maybe just a bit younger, I
fell in love for the first time. I felt it, sure. But I didn't understand
anything about what was happening to me. It was something new,
a completely unique feeling. I couldn't explain it; just experience
it. It was at once beautiful, turbulent, and even a bit confusing.

And as you might have expected—knowing my need for explanation—I started reading every book ever written on the nature of love. But ultimately I became my own experiment. I was
very aware of all the new feelings I was experiencing and how
uncontrollable they were. And I made a mental note about each
and every one of them.

I remember learning in some class (I don't remember which)
that Aristotle's idea of love was as a tendency toward the other.
This, more or less, explains the love that a couple feels, the love
between parents and children, and even the love we feel for ani-
mals and nature itself. Let's just say that it served me as something of a theoretical benchmark. But it's also a very cold and
distant concept, don't you think? I needed something that would
really touch me deeply.

Don't get me wrong: Besides being a student of love, I was
also a student in love.

So, half embarrassed and half confused by my sexual maturation and dominated by that need to define myself—to know
who I was and what I was feeling—I went looking for answers.
Remember, I was still basically a kid at this point who didn't even
need to shave yet. Despite the confusion of youth, I was pretty
sure about one thing: That in order to be in love with someone

else, first I had to love myself. Love itself is not enough. You have to be ready to receive it, you must be mentally prepared for someone to adore you.

One fortuitous day, a copy of Erich Fromm's *The Art of Loving* fell into my hands. I liked the idea that "egoism and self love, far from being identical, are actually complete opposites." The egoist is unable to love anyone other than himself. So, my theory of love was gaining some steam. But the theory had to be put into practice.

I was afraid of disappearing into my girlfriend's life, and equally weary of compelling her to give up her own interests and ambitions to be with me. The compromise would be a fragile and delicate balance. Later I read Kahlil Gibran, and things started to become clarified:

> *Love one another but make not a bond of love:*
> *Let it rather be a moving sea between the shores of your souls . . .*
> *And stand together, yet not too near together:*
> *For the pillars of the temple stand apart,*
> *And the oak tree and the cypress grow not in each other's shadow.*

Together and yet separate at the same time. Complicated, right?

I'll see if I can't simplify that just a bit. When I was younger, I was filled with dreams, plans, and itineraries. And I didn't want any relationship to change all that. I wanted to be on the move, not putting down roots. But that was also when I was discovering love for the first time: It was an unsettling feeling, and it had tied me to a person whom I didn't want to leave.

Somehow, I had to combine the two things. The question was how. I've yet to come up with a satisfactory answer, but I hope that I've gotten close. Love, then, is a way of growing as a person while being in the company of someone who supports you and whom you support, someone who admires you and whom you admire. It's a bilateral question, it's a wind blowing in two directions. It's incredibly complicated, and incredibly beautiful.

Every couple is a new experiment that—through the mixing—becomes something very different from its two original parts.

I've always believed that there is an element of admiration in love. Well beyond companionship, friendship, and physical love, mutual plans have to include admiration. Attraction is just a part of it. If you don't admire something about your partner, if there is not a quality about them that constantly lifts you up, that inspires you to be more than you thought you could, then the relationship runs the danger of sinking under the weight of minutiae.

> **If you don't admire something about your partner, if there is not a quality about them that constantly lifts you up, that inspires you to be more than you thought you could, then the relationship runs the danger of sinking under the weight of minutiae.**

I have been in love a few times. And I can tell you that there was nothing gradual about the process. Each time, it was like an explosion. And I never deigned to be a student of love. That would have been an incredible waste of time. I stepped right in it. It's true. My education in love was—like so many others—filled with ups and downs, as well as sheer madness. Who has ever been in love and not lost his head?

When you're in love, you think that there's nothing like it, and that nobody has ever had the same sort of experience as you.

That's why Francesco Alberoni, in his book *I Love You*, postulates that there is always something "extraordinary" in the state of love. And how could there not be something extraordinary about feeling new, connecting with someone, getting to know them deeply, and creating something together?

Love is "the experience of discovering a new world," as Alberoni says. Love is explosive, unique, it makes you feel alive, leaves other loves in the past, free, enlightening, looking to the future, "and the person whom you love is the doorway leading to all of this."

(Forgive my tendency to fall into the trap of overquoting, but I just want to show you a bit of what I've had the chance to see.)

The sweetest part of being in love is never having to worry that one day you'll be found out. You can look your partner in the eye and then look away without fear. You have nothing to hide. You're sincere and transparent to each other. Comfortably naked. There is a good deal of complicity in couples who love each other. Glances exchanged, gestures, and secret codes that only they can understand. Nobody else shares in them.

There is something magical in finding that exact dose of confidence, respect, humor, and attraction in your partner. If one of those elements is missing, or if the relationship isn't carefully balanced, the harmony can be broken. And you know what? I think that the relationships in which I've laughed the most have turned out to be the best ones. Perhaps it's from the fluidity and confidence implied by the ability to laugh and joke around with someone without worrying about embarrassment.

The joy of lasting love is that it evolves, changes, and continues to give in surprising ways. All healthy relationships must grow. When that growth becomes stunted, it's time for concern. The lights come on: attention! Arguments begin when agreements are not kept, or when one of the two partners begins to feel betrayed or overlooked.

I wish I could tell you otherwise, but not all marriages are lifelong commitments. If one or both partners find themselves falling out of love, then ending it may be for the best. I know a number of couples who didn't separate in time, and the long-term damage to all those involved is much greater than it could have been if the break had been made honestly and at the appropriate time.

~ **I wish I could tell you otherwise, but not all marriages are lifelong commitments. If one or both partners find themselves falling out of love, then ending it may be for the best.**

It hurts a lot. A whole lot. That much is for sure. "Ending a relationship is like dying," writes Igor Caruso in his classic book *Love and Separation.* There is pain, grief, and absence. Part of loving is letting love go. The counterpoint to love's euphoria is the desolation that comes when love is at an end. There is nothing more sad and alone than a lover who now finds himself alone. It feels like dying.

Both love and the absence of love can make you feel unique in the world, and they can both seem like things that will never end. Both are very intense feelings. They are a part of life. I don't want to give you the impression that life goes on unchanged after a divorce or a separation. It's just not the case. You and I both know that. Life doesn't go on the way it did before. But you adapt, and you reinvent yourself.

And maybe—because why not?—you fall in love again. Or, at the very least, learn to be better about loving those around

you—parents, siblings, and friends—even when it's very difficult.

There are times when families can drown us, right? I know it
happened to me. I loved my parents and my siblings very much,
but the routines of daily life together prompted my move toward
independence. I felt so trapped by the family dynamic and structure that my idea of liberty was a hotel room. Seriously. Hotels
gave me freedom. They were my space. Just for me. For twenty-
four hours, I didn't have to share them with anyone.

The great irony of my life is that I found myself feeling much
closer to my family when I went away to live in another country.
From a distance, I learned to love them more. Now I visit them
as often as I can, for my own peace of mind and to make up for
lost time. Once or twice a year, the whole Ramos family will
get together. And there's more than a bit of love at each of these
reunions.

One of the things that I've taken upon myself since I first
came to live in the United States over two decades ago is organizing our famous family reunions. Well, famous among ourselves. Memorable. As always, we attend them happily.

You've both experienced these events, where all my siblings
come with their children, where memories are hilariously recalled and many photo albums are brought out. Our family is
spread across the world. We have family in Jakarta, others in
Saltillo, and a few more in Madrid, Los Angeles, San Juan, and
Geneva. We, of course, live in Miami, and now you, Paola, are in
college in New York. We're on almost every continent.

It might sound glamorous, but in reality it takes a monumen-
tal effort to coordinate schedules and keep everyone in contact.
I love our family reunions; they are incredibly fun. It's not even
that we're a particularly happy family; for the most part, we are

reserved and sometimes overly serious. (And we like it that way. Thanks for asking!) But when we get together, it's a party. These reunions are something of a compensation for all the time we spend apart. They are where we share the love we've been saving.

Of course, they have the advantage of being brief. We can spend a day giving hugs, telling secrets, and even enduring the occasional bad mood, because—after all—it's only for a while. The drawback is having to wait until the next family reunion. There's a lot of nostalgia in those get-togethers. We struggled through so much pain before we finally realized that we haven't stopped loving one another even as life has distanced us from one another.

As I've told you, when I was young, I spent a large part of my time with my siblings, and the custom in our family—as it was with many Mexican families in those days—was to spend every weekend with grandparents, aunts, uncles, cousins, and close friends. Well, things have changed a bit. Today, few families— Latin American or otherwise—live in the same city. Moving is the norm, often for economic reasons or because you can't find the job you like in the city in which you live.

And we have been no exception.

So when we do get together, we are reminded of those weekends during our youth. I enjoy seeing my siblings, even though from time to time we'll sit down to dinner and exchange only a few words. I understand; it's our way of communicating, a way that we learned when we were still very young.

Our family dynamic was never terribly dynamic. When we sat down to dinner on the weekends—the only times during the week that we were all together: my parents, my three brothers, and my sister—there was a certain sense of solemnity hanging over the table. We used our silverware, we didn't shout or cry, we shared the food, and when everyone had finished eating, we helped clear the table. But we didn't have many meaningful discussions. No news. Our conversations didn't last long. After finishing our meals, the first thing we wanted to do was go out and play.

On a few very rare occasions, we would talk about sex, religion, or politics in the home. And it wasn't because my father prohibited such things or that they made my mother uncomfortable. The problem was that Grandpa Jorge was a man of few words, nor was he very accepting of any arguments contrary to his own opinions. Plus, he had a short temper. Those things combined to snuff out any interesting conversation.

It's not that your grandfather was an ogre. Far from it. He was a surprisingly kind and sweet man. But it was a lot of work to overcome the old, ridiculous stereotype that a man should impose his vision of the world on his family. So, dinnertime was for talking about nice, noncontroversial subjects, and internalizing anything that might be taken for confrontation or open affection.

Just look: One dinner is enough to see how a family functions.

I still remember my father's exaggerated reactions to any loud noise. The sound of a plate or a piece of silverware hitting the ground and his face would twist into such a look of distress that both terrified us and gave us something to laugh about behind his back.

I'm telling you this so that you might understand a bit more about why my family is so reserved. We learned at an early age not to share things with one another. Discussions risked my father's wrath. We didn't know how to air our differences without fear of a stern look or a shout ending the game. And—as always happens—you start to think that every family is like that.

But no.

Your aunt Carolina, so full of life and energy, will occasionally get frustrated with us and say to her husband, "Ger, why
don't you give your brother Jorge a hug? He loves you so much
and lives so far away." And she's right.

And, to be honest, via time and distance, we have learned to
loosen up. A bit. To love one another, to say it, and to express it.
Today there are more hugs, more declarations of fraternal love,
more awareness of the time we have left here in the second half
of life. And it's good. Really good.

As an adult, I had to work hard to break with the family dynamic that I'd learned as a child and that favored silence and
guardedness over engagement and emotions. It was hard to learn
how to talk to other people openly, consistently, without fear of a
scolding or other sign of disapproval.

My children, there are some things you learn during your
childhood before spending the rest of your life trying to unlearn
them. And I'm worried that the two of you will end up dragging
around some pending matters that you inherited from me. I apol-
ogize in advance. I hope that you can deal with them through
patience and a little forgiveness toward your old man. Because I
want to be there to discuss them with you, and I hope that you
will always know that I'm ready to talk with you about anything.
Anything at all. I don't want you to be afraid of me the way I once
was around my own father.

"I'm worried about my kids," said Patsy Loris a few days ago.
She's the executive producer for the station where I work, and
also one of my best friends. She had entered my office looking
very concerned. I thought for a moment that it was something
having to do with the news, but no. She wanted to talk about her
children.

"If something ever happened to one of them, I'd just die," she said, looking at the floor. "I just couldn't take it. I'd go crazy. What can we do to protect them?" Then she answered herself. "Nothing, right?" Patsy had just finished talking with a friend of hers who was facing a terrible problem with her twenty-five-year-old son. And I knew that she, as a mother, would have a sense of vulnerability all her life.

We worry about our children more than any other thing. Whenever something happens to them, it's as if it also happens to us.

I'll tell you a little story. When you were younger and, for example, you'd fall or stumble into something, a sort of electrical jolt would run through my body. It was a physical reaction, as if it was really me who had fallen.

And that still happens.

Nico, do you remember that awful night not too long ago that you spent with a fever, coughing, and vomiting? Well, when I was trying to help you get back to sleep, I started to experience the same symptoms that you were suffering, but it seemed to go beyond simple disease transmission. The bond between fathers and sons is a strange one, and explaining it defies simple logic.

And the way in which we suffer together is also the way we enjoy things together.

There's no doubt in my mind that our trips together, Paola, and those long weekends we spent, Nicolás, will be a part of my memories well into my later years.

You both are, literally, a part of me. And I wouldn't know how to live without you. It is, let's just say, a very different sort of love than the romantic and physical sort that I talked about at the beginning of this letter. It's totally and absolutely unconditional. There is no need to regain any balance or to negotiate any truces. It simply is.

Everything in my life revolves around you, just like it did with my mother and us. The circles continue to multiply.

Here there is no big mystery, no hidden secret. True, impartial love is found with your children. Everything else is, by nature, something less.

∽ **Here there is no big mystery, no hidden secret. True, impartial love is found with your children. Everything else is, by nature, something less.**

To love is to give you time, and my time is,
as it always has been, for both of you.
Papá

Letter 13

OF FAITH AND WILL

～

Love is my religion—I could die for it.

—JOHN KEATS

Kids:

I would like to believe in God, just like that, with a capital G, but I don't think I can.

When life is hard, the comfort of religion would be an immense help. At least I would have a whole set of answers to questions that I can't answer based on the history of others or my own experience. But believing is a question of faith and will. And I'm lacking in that faith, and unwilling to force it.

～ **But believing is a question of faith and will. And I'm lacking in that faith, and unwilling to force it.**

Everyone feels the need to find answers to the most basic of questions—Where do we come from? Where are we going? How does life begin? What happens after death? The answers religions offer are myriad and complex, yet no single scripture or spiritual leader has convinced me they hold the truth. I need answers to the questions that are spiritually satisfying to me, and the one size fits all declarations of most religions do not offer it.

Declaring that God exists is, for me, just as illogical as declaring that he doesn't exist. I have no way of proving or disproving this existence. At some level, many believers and atheists have at least this much in common: a sense of certainty. And an easy route to certainty is something I have never found. My training as a journalist has taught me always to look for reliable facts that can be confirmed by at least one (though preferably two) sources before making a declaration. And when it comes to matters of the divine, there are neither facts nor sources.

As such, I can only claim, for now, to be an agnostic. I just *don't know.* I feel much more in tune with the dictionary definition of agnosticism—"a person who holds the view that any ultimate reality (as God) is unknown and probably unknowable"—than I do with any of the arguments in favor of the existence of a god or gods. In my case, this is the most honest answer.

I have to admit that I'm surprised by and sometimes even a bit envious of those who have a rock-solid religious conviction. I'm sure that their lives are more peaceful than mine. And I have a deep respect for their religious beliefs and faith—many astounding acts of beauty and grace today and in history are directly attributable to those acting with a sincere belief in God, a belief that this entity acts on them to make the world a better, more tolerant, and more equitable place to live. They've simply reached a very different conclusion about the universe than I have.

Kids, you might think that I feel this way because of what I've seen of war, natural disasters, and terrorist attacks. And the truth is yes, those things have affected my outlook. But they're only part of the explanation. I believe there is no destiny, there is no plan. You have to make one for yourself. The world doesn't have a predetermined order, it doesn't follow just and fair rules, and things don't always happen for a reason. Humanity is not a divine experiment; it's a confrontation of wills, both collective and individual, without a predetermined end.

～ **The world doesn't have a predetermined order, it doesn't follow just and fair rules, and things don't always happen for a reason. Humanity is not a divine experiment; it's a confrontation of wills, both collective and individual, without a predetermined end.**

My religious doubts were established years ago. My adult life has simply reaffirmed them. When I was young, I just found Mass to be boring; when a little older, I was downright incredulous. I always resisted authority, whether it was wearing a cassock or not. To me, the supernatural elements combined with the head-shakingly absurd and frequently cruel rulebook endowed those who preached religion with an aura of lunacy.

Nevertheless—and I hope I don't fall into a contradiction here—I was in agreement with your grandparents who had you-baptized? Their religious beliefs are much stronger than mine, and someday the two of you may need them. The universe your relatives lived in is almost circular. It explains much more than mine does. And there are times in life when you need a sense of certainty, or even the ballast of ceremony, to grab on to. Your life with God will surely be more stable than mine is with doubt.

Your grandpa Jorge was a religious man who, near the end of his life, became even more so. Despite suffering a stroke and a number of heart attacks, he never lost his faith. He was convinced—

absolutely convinced—that after this life came another, better one. And his religious beliefs helped him a lot when he needed them the most. And honestly, I was grateful for that religious structure. The Catholic Church never explained much to me, but it gave my father a sense of protection and peace through to the end of his life.

I don't want to impose my views on you. I want you both to know that you're free to choose. It's for your own well-being. So when it comes to religion, I want you to come to your own conclusions. When you told us you wanted to take your first communion, Paoli, I supported you one hundred percent and flew to Madrid to share that very personal decision with you. It's very possible that—as has happened before—you made a better decision than I did.

I understand that I'm part of a misunderstood minority. And that it really is possible to doubt the existence of God and at the same time have a very strong inner life. I would almost go so far as to call it spiritual. But it's a connection with myself and with others who go beyond the physical plane. It occurs both when I'm concentrating in a Bikram yoga class, and when I'm sharing an intimate moment with my significant other. And it's perfectly normal to feel an unusual connection after helping less fortunate people. Solidarity and compassion are both parts of a meaningful inner life that doesn't have to depend on religion to be incredibly moving.

My prayers are based here on earth. They're never aimed at heaven. I want a healthier planet. Less crime. Less hunger. I want men and women to be equals on the street, in the office, in the churches, and in the schools. I aspire to the same things that any religious person would. The difference is that I don't ask anybody for them, or expect a prayer to magically be answered. My prayer is a plan of action, a strategy, an analysis of how to achieve what I want. That's the nature of my inner life.

⌐ My prayer is a plan of action, a strategy, an analysis of how to achieve what I want. That's the nature of my inner life.

I might even call it spiritual if I could separate my spirit from my body, if I could just figure out where the hell those twenty-one grams the soul is supposed to weigh are. But whenever I pinch myself to try and drive the spirit out of my body, all I get is blood and sweat. When I try and touch my soul, my skin shivers. And when I try and separate my mind and my brain, I get a headache.

It is indeed possible to live without religion. It's like letting yourself drift off without wearing a life jacket. It grants you a sense of freedom—I've found it's much easier to swim.

Like the old existentialists, I believe that life has no inherent meaning. You have to give meaning to it. And living without the absolute certainty of a deity or a life after this one is, of course, more worrisome. But I prefer it that way. It's my reality.

I love the present, and I urge myself to do as much as possible in the here and now. Because, for me, there is no later.

I believe in you,
Paola and Nicolás

FOR WHEN
I'M NO LONGER HERE

⌒

Kids, don't read this letter:

You can skip over it. It might be as hard to read as it was to write.

But I want to leave you something in writing for when I'm no longer here. Sooner or later, it's going to happen. This is a letter that you should store along with my will and testament and other important documents.

This is a map so that, during a time of hardship, you will know what your dad would do. You don't have to follow it to the letter; it's just a guide. A way of offering my hand, should you ever need it.

In fact, I'm not quite sure I understand this myself. I didn't leave you any written letters when I went off to cover wars; I suppose that, in some way, not leaving you a letter would oblige me to return safely. Maybe I feel more vulnerable now. Or now I'm able to express things that once had me all choked up. Perhaps it's all of the above.

You know what? I would have appreciated having a letter like this from my own father. I would have held on to it forever. Something to always remind me how important we were to him.

To begin, let me tell you how happy you kids have made me. More than I ever imagined. When I was young, I thought that I wouldn't want any children—the egoism typical of a teenager who thought there wouldn't be time for everything he wanted to do. Plus, taking care of children didn't fit into my limited idea of freedom.

Then I met you, and everything changed. Your births opened a giant hole in my steel armor, blowing away any of my youthful fears or concerns. I learned very quickly that being a father was the best thing that could ever have happened to me.

Thanks, Pao. Thanks, Nico.

Now I understood my freedom perfectly, understood how it includes the power to love someone to the fullest. Loving the two of you has made me more free than ever. It's opened me up emotionally. Saved me from an incomplete life.

Many years ago, a good friend of mine who had left the field of journalism to dedicate herself to a spiritual life told me that my daughter would be my salvation, that she would keep me connected to myself and to the feelings of others. And she was right. Nico, you weren't born yet, but we can say the exact same thing about you.

I've had a good life. I have no complaints. In general, things have turned out better than I ever imagined. When I was a teenager, I had so many plans, so many places to go, so many things to do. And life has given me even more. I've been able to live the life I wanted. Nobody chose it for me . . . I'm both to blame and happily responsible for everything I've either done or haven't done.

Which, I understand, has had its inconveniences. I've lived with so much intention, always analyzing why I do what I do, that I occasionally feel a certain density of existence. It's like when you say to me, "Relax, Daddy, relax." You're right. I could stand to loosen up a little bit. I could stand to loosen up *a lot*.

I've wasted a lot of time following formats and protocols and uniforms. And (as Borges might say) if I could live it all over again, I would have more fun and take fewer things so seriously. I might try and have a little more fun.

You should have fun.

One of the things I realized when you were babies was that I would be playing a lot with you. My father almost never played with me, and I didn't want to repeat that mistake. Nothing makes me happier. Somehow, playing together makes all three of us the same age, and that feeling is unlike any other. There is just nothing more sweet or anything more important than horsing around and spending time with you. I wouldn't trade a moment of it. I only regret that which we didn't do. Never what we did. So you should never be afraid to try new things. You can't return an un-lived life to the store.

Experiment with (almost) everything, learn something new.

The day you stop learning is the day you start getting old. And I'm still learning things from you. It wasn't too long ago that you two taught me how to snowboard and how to score on your soccer video game. It wasn't easy. I ended up covered in bruises and frustrated at the fact that the little men on the screen wouldn't do what I wanted them to do. But it was worth all that to learn two new things.

Spend time with people who challenge you, who make you

think, who don't put you to sleep. Dare to be young, even when
your face and your body tell you otherwise.

Don't slink into corners—overcome shyness.

🌙 **Spend time with people who challenge you, who make you
think, who don't put you to sleep. Dare to be young, even
when your face and your body tell you otherwise.**

Don't slink into corners—overcome shyness.

The three of us are often hesitant. I know. It's hard for us
to ask for things, call attention to ourselves, or inconvenience
others. But you have to get over it. How will you know whether
something can be achieved if you haven't even tried? The first
step is always the most intimidating. Look. Do. Get involved. Immerse yourself in life.

There are no substitutes for swimming in the ocean; laughing
so hard that you give yourself a headache; sleeping with someone
you love; breathing the air on a snowcapped mountain; dipping
your feet in a river; walking down the streets of New York, Paris,
Mumbai, or Mexico City after a sunshower; watching a movie
that makes you cry and think; watching your favorite actors on
the London, Madrid, or Buenos Aires stage; eating tacos from a
street vendor; sleeping in the nude; skiing for the first time; publishing something you've written; flying a kite in Bangkok; taking an afternoon siesta; devouring a pineapple with chile piquín;
feeling mud squish between your fingers—so give a lecture, be
on television, lose yourself in a tiny little town, take a nap in
a hammock, go three days without taking a shower, take three
showers in one day, splash some warm water on your face when
you're dying of thirst, sweat in a steam bath, dive as deep as you
can under water, ride a bicycle through a vineyard, play Ping-

Pong, roll down a sand dune in Veracruz, get a sunburn on your cheeks in the late afternoon . . .

Travel. A lot.

This has been my only luxury, my favorite prize, and my best reward. I've never been completely disappointed by a trip. There is always something to be gained.

Go see new and different things. If a place makes you feel somewhat uncomfortable, it's because there's something uncomfortable inside of you. Something that needs to be adjusted or reflected upon. And don't leave that place until you understand what it is that's moving inside of you.

～ **Go see new and different things. If a place makes you feel somewhat uncomfortable, it's because there's something uncomfortable inside of you. Something that needs to be adjusted or reflected upon. And don't leave that place until you understand what it is that's moving inside of you.**

That's why you've come with me on so many trips. I don't want you to stop moving. There is no reason to stand in one corner when there is a whole wide world out there to explore. Every new place opens up a door inside of you. If you can, visit one new country every year. By the time you're eighty, you'll have covered a good part of the globe. Stay away from those cruises that keep you holed up in their own little world and where all meals are included. Get out of there. Go ride a bike around Beijing. Snorkel on the Great Barrier Reef. Spend a few days in an ashram in India. Keep your eyes open while you close off that little part of your mind telling you that your world is better. Don't judge. Participate. Fill the planet.

Don't live with fear.

It paralyzes you. It's normal to feel fear from time to time, but you have to handle it like a barking dog. It can stop you in your tracks, but you can also control it; it's just a noise, an alarm, a call to action.

Take three deep breaths, understand what's happening inside you—that fear is welling up in the pit of your stomach and the lump in your throat—and then push the fear aside. Give a name—both first and last, if you have to—to your fear. Repeat that name several times, and you'll start to see its power decline. It runs out of energy. You have to identify your opponent before you can ultimately defeat it. And remember this: Most of your enemies exist within.

So, take risks.

When I was still in high school, a group of friends and I decided to publish a newspaper that was highly critical of both the school and its teachers. Of course, we were running the risk of being expelled. The school was no democracy, and freedom of expression—particularly when it was directed at the teachers and administrators—was not well received.

But before we did so, we consulted with one teacher who appreciated our nerve. We learned that expression of dissent could cost us a whole year of schooling. We didn't know quite what to do, but we did know a way to measure the risk. "If the reward is greater than the possible punishment, then let's do it."

Ultimately, we decided to publish the paper. All the students and teachers at the school read it . . . and nothing happened. No expulsions, no punishments. But the experience taught us something even more important. The school was no longer doing anything for us. Several of the students who had helped to publish the manifesto transferred to a different school the next year. Before I left, I had the pleasure of looking the director in the face and telling him, "I'm leaving because I'm not going to take it anymore."

I ended up at a much more liberal school, one more in tune with my way of thinking. And it's also quite possible that that experience helped determine my chosen profession. After all, the reward turned out to be much more impressive than the risk. I can only hope that, had there been a negative outcome, my friends and I would have handled the consequences gracefully.

Don't be a victim.

If, for whatever reason, you find yourself victimized, then fight back. Being a victim means losing control of your life. Fight with everything you've got to get back in control. Nobody has the right to tell you how to live your life. And living as a victim isn't really living at all.

You are responsible for your actions. That's it. Never blame others for something you've done. Ever. It's a cowardly way of living. We are responsible both for what we do and what we don't do. Every decision we make has long-term consequences. And we have to learn to accept this. That way, you'll be able to live a clean, open life. There's nothing more satisfying than knowing that you've lived a life according to your own terms.

And if you're ever faced with the unfortunate experience of being victimized by something completely out of your control, have the courage to forgive yourself. Not everything is under your control. You don't have to carry the weight of the world upon your shoulders. You do not have to take responsibility for everything.

You must learn when to say no.

Sometimes, the decision to say no is the hardest and most courageous decision you can make. When I turned forty, I gave myself the gift of saying no. And it was the best thing I've ever given myself. I told myself that, from that point on, I would say no to the things that I didn't wholeheartedly want to do. I would go to fewer compulsory events. I would simply say no more often. It took a lot of work, but—after a few years—I got the hang of it. It freed me up.

I don't let people pressure me into things. Sometimes it can be hard to turn them down, but in the end, it's better to have said no at the start than to carry the resentment of having said yes for years afterward. It's a bit of proactivity you won't regret.

Take action.

This is certainly one of the principal lessons that I've learned: It's better to be active than to be passive. It's better to treat something than to wait and hope. There is no room in life for "could've, should've, would've." Nothing generates more frustration and resentment than never having tried.

"We must always take sides," said Elie Wiesel, author of the book *Night*, which describes the atrocities he bore witness to while imprisoned in a Nazi concentration camp. "Neutrality helps the oppressor, never the victim. And action is the only remedy to indifference, the most insidious danger of all."

It's never wrong to denounce an injustice or to confront someone abusing their position or power. It might not be easy, but life is too short to walk around neutral. Don't be afraid to defend your ideals. It takes strength of character, and it's to be praised.

In those complicated situations where it seems like there is no way to choose, there is a simple rule you can use: Don't ever compromise your principles. Don't simply take the easy or comfortable way out. You have to assure yourself that after making an important decision, you'll still be able to look yourself in the mirror, and self-respect is more precious than you can imagine.

You're going to have to live with that face for the rest of your life. Take a deep breath, and think.

Make big decisions calmly.

∿ Make big decisions calmly.

We're making decisions all the time. It's part of living freely. Once in a while the choice is so difficult, and the stakes are so high, it can send us into panic mode. These big decisions are ones that will affect us for the rest of our lives. They have to be made with complete awareness of their significance. In my life, the biggies included the decision to come here to the United States. Another when I decided to become a journalist. The most important was when I finally decided to become a father. All of these choices will affect every waking moment of my life until the day I die.

Be sure that when it comes time for the two of you to make these kinds of decisions, you do so in a completely calm manner. Deep down, they're actually some of the easiest ones to make. They're products of many years of maturation, and you'll have the experience to make them.

Big decisions—like choosing a partner, country, career, or parenthood—often have an air of inevitability about them. They'll come to you naturally, in time. If it's any other way, be careful and always think twice. Don't wait a decade or more to correct a bad decision. Don't waste your energy.

And I know it's a cliché, but don't sweat the small stuff.

It's just not worth the time and energy to worry about trivial matters. Let them go. You don't have to fight and win every single argument. Learn to separate what's important from what isn't. Gauge your strength and save it for things that have a real effect on your life and the lives of those around you. You don't always have to be first in line. You'll get there when it's time.

That said, watch your timing.

A kiss at just the right moment is resplendent; a kiss at the wrong time can wind up with a slap in the face. I began to understand the fine tuning it takes to reach these somewhat elusive opportune moments when I was a summer camp counselor. I took advantage of the nights, just before the campers were bedded down for the evening, to talk to them about their fears and aspirations. Everything carries greater weight—advice, an embrace, a chat, a confession, a complaint—if it's done at the appropriate time and place.

Sometimes waiting a bit can ultimately have a greater impact. Even if you're feeling the moment—a funeral isn't the place for a marriage proposal, and a carnival isn't the place to remember those who have left us.

I'll tell you a story about an encounter that taught me much and that still hurts to recall. When I was a child, there was a priest at school who always played with us and who always treated us with kindness and respect. Even though he wore a cassock, he was our friend. He taught first- or second-grade classes (I don't recall exactly), was the only one who played soccer during recess, and was the only padre to whom we could confess our mischievousness without fear of being reprimanded.

Anyway, Father Sergio—for reasons I could take a guess at, though I don't know for sure—left the religious life and went to live in New York. And on one fine day, some thirty years after I'd last seen him, he got in touch with me by sending a letter to my office. He'd seen me on television and wanted to get back in touch.

I was happy to hear from the now former father Sergio; plus, it would give me an unique opportunity to do some mental and emotional cleanup from those days. There were a thousand questions I wanted to ask him. I looked through some of my old photo albums, and there was Sergio, in black and white, serious and vigilant, there with his students. Close. Accessible.

I had wanted to wait for the right moment to ask all the lingering, bothersome questions from that time and place. And as that moment was slow in coming, I left things hanging and postponed responding to his letter. It wasn't that I'd forgotten about it—his letter was right there on my desk—but my childhood issues were so important that I was only able to write down my questions a bit at a time.

Finally, three or fours months later, I had finally written a letter I was satisfied with. I didn't ask all the questions that I had. I thought that it would be better just to get in touch with Sergio and then sit down with him, face to face, perhaps in New York. I sent the letter and got no response from him.

Some six months after his first epistolary contact, I got another letter. But it wasn't from him. It was from an old college classmate, informing me that Sergio had died. My heart froze over. I felt a terrible emptiness inside. His friend mentioned that Sergio didn't talk much about his former students, but he did on occasion mention that he was pleased to see my professional accomplishments. That part made me cry.

From that moment on, I promised myself that I would act in a timely fashion when there was no guarantee I could afford to dillydally. Opportune moments occasionally demand swift action. In fact, I've learned that any sort of delay when it comes to truly important matters is a bad idea. They require—and deserve—immediate attention. Dragging things out only adds noise to your life. That was the last thing that Sergio ever taught me. Only too late.

Second chances are few and far between.

You already know that I don't believe in destiny or luck. Instead, I believe in preparing yourself for when opportunities present themselves. When it happens, jump on it. But you must be prepared.

Successful people aren't necessarily the ones who are the most intelligent. Sometimes, they're just the most persistent. If they truly want something, it shows. And they translate that desire into time and energy. They dedicate themselves to their cause. They don't waste time doing things that other people think they should be doing; they find their own true passion in life and sink their teeth into it.

Don't live a life without passion.

There's nothing sadder than spending your life doing something you don't enjoy. Choose something that changes you, that challenges you. Money and comfort will come in time. And if they don't, it's not important. It's better to live your life doing something you want to do rather than something else that involves money, comforts, and boredom.

Use the money you earn, but don't let the money you earn use you.

It's no big secret that I've tried to give you the things that I never did—the trips I never took, the academic opportunities that I never had, the peace of mind that comes from being untroubled by constant money woes. Economic self-sufficiency allows you more freedom when it comes to making decisions. And that freedom is the only thing that you should covet. Accumulating stuff will only hinder you and drag you down. Personally, I'm more of a minimalist. Just take a peek inside my house or closet.

I live well, which is just a way of saying that I provide for my needs. The United States has been tremendously generous to me. And, in return, I hope that the two of you will be generous to those who need it most. That's all. Okay?

Dialogue can solve everything.

I don't like fighting. All wars are proof of failed dialogues. To me, there is no such thing as a good or just war. I prefer building bridges. And to do that, you have to be able to listen. I'm a pretty good listener. They say that good speakers come from good listeners. You have to know how to be the latter before you can be the former.

With you, I've always tried to erase the idea of off-limits topics. It's the first rule of free and unprejudiced conversation. "Because I said so" is a phrase that can derail any conversation. Everything has to be laid out on the table. And if you feel confident enough to talk about any subject with me, then the strength gained and the lesson learned will have been well worth the effort.

Be transcendent.

Go beyond yourselves. Leave your mark. Don't sneak through life without being noticed. We're not responsible for the state of the world when we enter it, but we have an obligation to leave it a little better off by the time we exit it. Once, when you were both very young, I thought that I wanted to save the world. And there's nothing wrong in believing that one single person can change things. Don't ever lose that sense of idealism. Love your dreams. Great changes begin in the imagination.

Be leaders.

Don't be afraid to state your opinion and to propose your ideas. There are six billion other people out there doing the same thing. So when you're convinced about something, speak up about it. It's always better to lead than to follow. And if you fall, at least you'll be able to say that nobody pushed you.

> ⌣ It's always better to lead than to follow. And if you fall, at least you'll be able to say that nobody pushed you.

Remember, life doesn't come with sense included. You have to add it yourself. The best way to gain sense and wisdom is by giving something to the people around you. Just look up and you'll see that there's a lot you can do. Think big but first take a short walk. My preference is to scoot around consensus, even if my detour makes my walk a little more winding.

Be independent.

Independence—both economic and intellectual—is a requirement of a genuine, authentic life. Independence is my main asset and also my worst liability. Sometimes I act alone when, in fact, it would have been better to let myself receive some help, and I recognize that I have to work at adapting myself to making more collective decisions.

Of course, I don't mean that life is better without any strong emotional ties to other people. I depend on the love of my family and friends in much the same way as you depend on my love and the love of those around you. Be self-sufficient in all ways except when it comes to love. Any other way of doing it would be quite a bore.

Be yourselves. If, for some reason, you forget everything I've ever said to you up to this point, then remember this: Be yourselves.

Well, I think I've given you a few answers to the question of "What would Dad have done?" But at the end of the day, don't give it too much thought. Please. It's your life, after all. Not mine.

And when I'm no longer here, don't worry. In many, many ways, you'll be carrying me with you. You just have to pay a little bit of attention, and you'll see me there. I love you both.

Everything is everything,
Dad

LIFE WITHOUT A WATCH

⌁

Clocks slay time . . . time is dead as long as it is
being clicked off by little wheels; only when the
clock stops does time come to life.

—WILLIAM FAULKNER

Paola and Nicolás:

This is the last letter that I'm writing to you. I hope that the
letters have been able to communicate the truly incredible way
in which you've changed my life and—at the same time—helped
you to get to know me just a little bit better. I'm sure we'll have
the opportunity to discuss these letters. Maybe the next time
you're stuck in the car with me . . .

I want to end this collection by talking a little bit about time.
The common thread running through these fifteen letters has
been the time that we've spent together. I'd like to lengthen it,
stretch it, draw it out. But I can't.

Life is composed of those snippets of time that stubbornly resist being saved, slowed down, speeded up, extended, or trimmed.
They are what they are.

What I would like most is to take a bit of my own dad's life and fit it like a piece of a puzzle into a part of your own life, Nicolás, so that he could watch you playing soccer on Saturday mornings. Or grab a slice of my old college basketball practices so that I could play with you, Paola, both of us at twenty years old. Or make a kiss last forever. Or cut out the pain of a blow. Or freeze those moments when I saw each of you for the very first time. But I can't. They're gone.

Memory guards such information, even though we can't ever see it live again. Sometimes I'll play around like I'm a film editor and splice together incongruent moments in time. In my movie, I'd like to include all those people who have touched my life in some way, everyone I love and who loves me. After all, isn't that the idea of heaven, where you can live eternally with those you love? I already know how mine will look.

The problem is that I don't necessarily believe that heaven exists. So I continue on, searching for my heaven here on earth. The lines in these letters and the gray hairs on my head are the proof of an intense recollection. Man, I'd really like to look five or ten years younger. Who wouldn't? But I know that every year has brought me something new: its lessons, a bit more experience, a bit less rigidity. That's why I carry signs of the passage of time like awards. I don't want to go back in time. I'm fine where I'm at. Plus, it's a privilege to be here with you when others, sadly, are not.

The best reward is living the life you chose and no other. It's liberating. Finally, I have the ability and knowledge to truly enjoy every moment of it. It's something I wasn't able to do before. I don't want to hide the time I've already spent because it would be like hiding my most precious gift.

The Spanish journalist Vicente Verdú wrote that one of the new luxuries of the twenty-first century would be "more and more time. For example, being able to watch flowers or plants or the movements of a child without needing to check your watch." He was right. I can't recommend living with a watch strapped to my wrist. I've never worn one or really any jewelry, for that matter. The passage of time is already being charted in so many other places, from cell phones to laptop computers.

Even the richest and most powerful men and women in the world are paupers in the face of time. I try not to attempt to control time, it's too exhausting and fruitless an endeavor. Instead, I like to enjoy time bit by bit, with you and other people I love, doing things that make me feel happy and light.

It's age—not Einstein—that teaches us that time is relative. When we were children, a week seemed like an eternity, and Christmas vacation seemed to come only once a century. Now, our birthdays come so quickly that they seem more like cars whizzing by at a NASCAR or F1 race. They gain speed with every lap, and there's no stopping them.

For a man who has lived half a century like I have, the perception of a year is very different than it is for an eight-year-old boy like you, Nicolás. For me, that year flies by. On the other hand, to you it seems interminable. Sometimes we might even want to trade, right? You want to speed up time, while I'd fancy slowing it down a bit—impossible either way.

If the speedy passing of time didn't affect me so much, I would have postponed writing these letters. Not to mention this reflection on some of my most favorite moments. Like the times (have you noticed?) that can encompass everything, and when your feet just fall into place. Just the other day, I had one such moment.

We were playing soccer in the yard, Nicolás, and the afternoon was just perfect: We were under a continuous orange and blue sky, neither hot nor cold, neither hungry nor thirsty, no lingering concerns or places to be, friends and family were well, with you shooting on goal with me trying to make saves, when suddenly I paused for a fraction of a second to recognize that everything was in its time and place, and at that moment—at that precise instant—I was incredibly happy.

Kids, I wish many such moments for you.

I don't know what's coming. Milan Kundera has said that "the whole world is mistaken about what is to come." But you have to take advantage of the time that you have and, lately, I've been very sensitive to the idea that life is constricted by a lack of it. Not long ago, lost among a mountain of photographs, I found a card from my friend Félix Sordo, who died in the earthquake in Mexico back in 1985. One of Félix's favorite expressions was "I'm in a hurry." And he wasn't referring to the present, to the fact that there is—or was—so much to do, but rather to that particular feeling that life is getting away from us, and that you have to move quickly in order to take care of everything. Yes, Félix, you lived quickly and because of that, you left your mark on many of us.

Also not long ago, I found an old magazine in which Elena Poniatowska discussed her eternal struggle with time: "I am in turmoil, as I have no time."

I feel the same way. I feel like I need more time. But since I can't give myself more, technically, at least I think I've found the formula for taking more advantage of it. Instead of rushing to get more things done in a shorter amount of time, I'm going to slow life down so that I can enjoy every moment that much more.

Multi-tasking is asking to be multi-unhappy. There's no proper method, but I try doing just one thing at a time. I try to eat without reading, talk without watching TV, make phone calls without working on the computer, attend parties without checking my BlackBerry, leave without looking at the time, sleep without an alarm clock, make love without music.

Less speed, less work, and less intensity. And you know what? It's working. It's life without a watch.

Now, more than ever, I understand the enormous privilege of being together. The true gift is the time we share, taking advantage of every moment we have left. In a manner of speaking, we're in overtime.

The two of you are the best of me. Even if there is no life after death, living with you has been worth everything to me. The time I've spent with you—those collected bits of shared moments—are the high point of my life.

The two of you are the best of me. Even if there is no life after death, living with you has been worth everything to me. The time I've spent with you—those collected bits of shared moments—are the high point of my life.

With you, Paola,
With you, Nicolás,
Always,
Jorge

THE PICTURE

If I could freeze one moment in time, it would be the one when we took that picture of the three of us. We were in Vail, Colorado, unhurried, without any particular plan, and not knowing what was going to happen next. We wanted to go home, to the warm weather of Miami, but our flight had been canceled. A storm had prevented our plane from landing, and it would be several hours before we could board another one. So we wandered around with the sun in our faces, a true gift there in the cold winter morning. We saw a store with the wonderful name of "Laughing Monkey," and we sat down on its steps to take this picture.

Nicolás had left his winter jacket in his suitcase, so I loaned him mine. It was a little big on him. But it gave us both a little bit of comfort: to him, from wearing one of his father's jackets, and to me, from that uncontrollable parental need to protect . . . even though I was freezing to death myself. And Paola, always the coolest one of all, with her scarf, her hair band, smiling away without any concern in the world.

There we were, the three of us, immensely happy.

Click.

Yes, I've squeezed a lot out of life . . . and life has been good to me.